KNOW THYSELF

KNOW THYSELF

Praise for Gian Kumar's Books

Having found inner peace, he (the author) reinforces his belief that knowledge is the greatest to mankind as he imparts his experiential learning in an attempt to inspire others to find meaning in their lives as well.

– Free Press Journal

This book is written after a wide research on the subject and hence its validity cannot be doubted. What is good about this book is that it does not give any moral lessons. It just tells you in a rational way about your infinite potential to find your ultimate state of bliss and peace.

This book encourages people to go beyond the realm of peace into the realm of science. We human associate ourselves with our thoughts. Thus I come into existence. It restricts us from connecting with the world. Our consciousness lies beyond our ego. It creates a sense of oneness with all. It does not look at itself as a separate entity. It looks at itself in union with the universe. Hence the author suggests some paths of yoga to reach this stage. This has been also suggested by other authors in their books on spirituality.

– Afternoon Voice

In the first of his series of 3 books -Know Thyself, Think from The Heart and The Ultimate Reality, Gian Kumar answers some of the most pressing spiritual questions

– DNA

As you peruse the extensive elaborations of the self herein, regarding knowledge, awareness and realization, you will surely find the help needed in transforming your life to reach the fullness and completion you yearn for and deserve. The Gian Kumar explains it all - The truer self lies within. it needs courage to be coaxed out, accepted and loved. "I could do it," he says and raises a question: Can you?

– Mumbai Messenger

Gian Kumar answers our questions related to spirituality in a simple and seamless manner. The core of this series is based upon the absolute reality of life-oneness between the self and the universe.

– The Asian Age

So you feel you truly know yourself? Well, you can get hold of the book - Know Thyself and have an insightful journey to discover your true self. It is an amalgamation of the author's knowledge and thoughts in science, spirituality and philosophy. A worth read!

– Planet Powai

From time immemorial, people have searched for definitive responses to questions such as: Who am I, where do I come from and does God exist? What is the essence of my relationship with him? Know Thyself by Gian Kumar attempts to answer such philosophical questions in a reader-friendly format.

– Society Magazine

Know Thyself is a book by inquisitive thinker. Born in Burma to a religious Hindu family and raised by traditional principles Gian Kumar is a deep, inquisitive thinker who moved towards spirituality after struggling with his curiosity regarding God and his purpose of existence. Spirituality provided him with a framework or morality and helped him become a better person.

– Trinity Mirror

KNOW THYSELF

BOOK I

Unravelling the mystery of the Mind

GIAN KUMAR

CELESTIAL BOOKS

Times Group Books

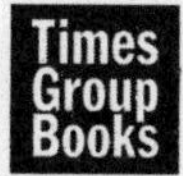

Know Thyself

Unravelling the mystery of the Mind

ISBN 978-93-52013-72-2

Layout: Ajay Shah
Cover Design: Deepanshu Rishi
Printed in India by Nutech Print Services - India

First Published in English in 2015 by:

An imprint of
Leadstart Publishing Pvt Ltd
Unit 25, Building A/1, Near Wadala RTO,
Wadala (E), Mumbai 400 037, INDIA
T + 91 96 9993 3000 E info@leadstartcorp.com
W www.leadstartcorp.com

This edition is reprinted in 2018.

Marketed & Distributed by:

A division of
Bennett, Coleman & Co.Ltd.

The Times of India, 10 Daryaganj, New Delhi - 110002
Phone: 011 - 39843333 Email: tgb@timesgroup.in
www.toibooks.com

To All Spiritual Beings.

About the Author

Gian Kumar was born into a traditional Hindu family, in Burma (present-day Myanmar). From childhood, his life held paradoxes which he struggled to understand. While he was educated at a Christian boarding school which observed strict religious practices, these were diametrically opposed to the Hindu traditions and customs which were the norm when he went home for the holidays.

A thinker by nature, the inherent confusion and dogmas underlying religion, gradually impelled him towards spirituality. Today, he is deeply grateful for a journey filled with opportunities to learn about existential riddles such as: *Who am I? What is my purpose in Life? Is God an illusion?* Gian hopes to share his own experiential learnings with others through the medium of his books.

Gian lives with his family in New Delhi. He can be reached at: giankumar@ymail.com

---

Book I Know Thyself
Book II Think From The Heart
Love From The Mind
Book III The Ultimate Reality

Editor's Note

Repetitions, in the spiritual context, are unavoidable since the concepts are infinite while the words to describe them remain pitifully finite. In this series, the author has constantly used concepts and words such as the Absolute, Oneness, Energy, Self and so on. Besides intellectually, the author has considered the reader's need to understand and absorb the subject, step by step. Hence, the core ideas being repeated at each juncture, helps the message to be distilled and internalized, instead of remaining partially understood.

It does not necessarily follow that the reader agrees with everything written. When the mind becomes impatient or restless, signaling it has understood, the reader should move on. The subjects/chapters often revolve around one word such as 'awareness' or 'oneness', which stand like the basic scale a classical *raga* is based on. Thereupon, a myriad variations and nuances are played, to attempt to convey the numerous extensions possible within the same theme.

The serious seeker of spiritualism returns by compulsion, to read again and again and hear those notes as a recurring melody, until the theme becomes clear. Like chanting a *mantra,* he then gains the proper perspective to practice what he has read.

Contents

Foreword

Who can know children better than their parents, and parents better than their children? Hence, I am perhaps the right person to write the foreword for this book by my father. I also think it should be about him.

Through the journey of life, we all meet and engage with a variety of people. Some are like beacons of light, some fail to leave an imprint, and others are there to ensure we continue to know the meaning of doubt. In my own life, whenever the going has been rough or I fall into serious self-doubt, I have always relied on my beacon of light – my father.

Whatever challenges life threw at him, he always emerged stronger. He lost his own father at a very young age, faced financial hardships, and struggled to set up his business. In doing so, he embraced every challenge and developed a unique and interesting perspective on life, which has been a source of inspiration and greater understanding for many people who have come into contact with him.

This book is an attempt to spread his philosophies far and wide. He shares with his readers his learning and experiences, but most of all, himself. I have benefitted manifold from these offerings on spiritual living and I hope others gain from them as much as I have. Not that our own lives teach us less, but our daily routines are usually so hectic that most people lack the energy or inclination to think beyond the everyday. As a result, we sometimes forget the wider world and many others, who like us, travel through life without having understood what we really are.

Everyone, at some point, needs a guide who can help us truly understand the self, what we seek, and how to achieve it. From personal experience I have found that whenever I sought answers from self-help or spiritual books, the Internet, gurus, etc., I have been left confused and dissatisfied, since what they preached often lacked the practical perspective of my own life or was just too complicated for a lay person to understand.

This book outlines, in the most simple way possible, philosophies about life which have emerged from the personal experience and spiritual practice of the most practical person I know; someone who has actually lived and gone through the phases and questions many of us are going through. His down-to-earth perspective on life's issues has served to largely remove my personal doubts and fears.

I suggest you read this book whenever you have the time for reflection, leafing through it again and again whenever in self-doubt. You will always find something to touch you, just as I have experienced. Good luck my fellow travellers, on this, our common journey of life!

C.A. Nadisha Kumar Gulati
Entrepreneur

Preface

When life is submerged in the trappings of materialism and existence revolves around me, mine and myself, we experience the hollow feeling that all that is ours today is ephemeral – both the emotional and the material.

There exists an emptiness, which we cannot define, a feeling of incompleteness. We wonder what we really want from life. Questions trouble the mind and we begin seeking new directions. We crave the true meaning of life, in its totality.

Every phase of life requires change. Questions such as: Who am I? Where have I come from? Where do we go? and many more, led me on my personal quest to discover the ultimate truth about life. Having found some measure of peace and understanding, I felt the need to share my experiential findings with others, under the umbrella of spiritualism.

We are each linked, yet separated, with many thoughts leading along the same path of existence, life, religion, spirituality and God. Here, I have attempted to cover every aspect of life within the ambit of spiritualism in the most accessible manner possible. This narrative carries the strong influence of ancient Eastern scriptures and philosophies, which I feel are as relevant today as when they were first formulated.

As you peruse the extensive elaborations in these three volumes, based on self-knowledge, self-awareness, and self-realization, I hope they help in transforming your life to reach the fullness and completion we all yearn for.

Gian Kumar
New Delhi, 2014

In a gentle manner, be a gentleman;
gently dissolve the 'I, me, mine and myself'
roaring within you.

Chapter 1
Knowing the Truth

It all started ten years ago. I was galloping along at a crazy pace in my life, making money and fascinated by the material comforts wealth provides. In everybody's life, a time comes when that fascination dims and we ask: now what? All sorts of questions regarding my style of living pointed me in the direction of the endless road I now find myself travelling upon. The real meaning and purpose of life began to dawn upon me. I felt deeply that there was a limit to every phase we go through. I craved understanding about what exactly life was and my purpose beyond those never-ending desires, selfish attachments and excessive accumulations.

I pondered what to do – whether to go towards religion or continue as I was, submerged in the various intoxicants of life. I kept asking myself why was it that I wanted more and more? Why was I not content? What was the reason for my insecurity and the shallowness of my existence?

How does one go about gaining a stable mind and body? Who was I really? Where did I come from? Why should I believe in God? Do we really need Him? Question after question kept pouring into my mind, driven by my lifestyle and my own uncertainties about life. Despite friends and family, I was lonely; despite wealth and property, there was emptiness within.

Having been an independent and strong-willed person throughout my life, I ventured on my quest alone, without seeking help – to search for, know and understand the completeness, which had eluded me for so long. Slowly, step-by-step, I started to climb up the tree of life, awakening to the truth, through self-discovery. It was not what religion had been preaching or what science declared. I had to discover the power of the spirit, the real me, which I was so ignorant about. My quest was to find my own truth, so that I could understand and experience what the seers, preachers and gurus preached.

But did their truth resonate with my own intellect, intentions and intuition, so that I too, could *experience* truth and not merely listen to what others called Truth? And you, reader-seeker, despite carefully perusing my three books, may still not achieve the spirit, truth and reality I have taken pains to elaborate upon because no knowledge is complete without experience and participation.

We know how much effort and research is required to acquire the knowledge which reveals the truth about life. The subject is both paradoxical and complex. Is truth subjective or objective? Is it relative or absolute? My own quest and discovery led me to write these books. Spiritualism can be defined in one word: Oneness. But it took me five years, three books and over 100,000 words to elaborate the secrets behind the truth of oneness. There are many chapters you may want to read more than once in order to capture the real essence of what is being communicated. And, for the same reason, you will find some of the explanations repeated several times. It has been done intentionally for better clarity.

Spiritualism, spirituality and spiritual practices have their own connotations and meanings for different people. They can be connected to religion, science, philosophy, psychology, and personal development. What is relevant here is what we consider to be true. Awakening our existential and experiential self to what is true and of value to us is far more preferable than blindly following the lofty ideals of gurus.

Many religions regard spirituality as an integral part of their practices. Science too, has begun to embrace certain concepts of spirituality, like that of everything being one energy. Spirituality is meant to develop a person's inner being; the goal – a more comprehensive self. Religion, on the other hand, is composed of various faiths, traditions, cultures and superstitions, bending with each towards separate, supernatural gods. While spirituality and religion finally merge into one thought, their directions and practice are very different.

Today, scientists, physicists and neuroscientists consider science and spirituality to be complementary, not contradictory. They are researching how the brain functions during spiritual experiences and what happens after one dies. Science has its own way of proving all that it can, objectively, while spiritualism delves into the meaning of life subjectively. Both science and spirituality are essential to human beings.

These pages reflect my own understanding of the subject-object relationship regarding the essence of life. Daniel Patrick Moynihan said, "Everybody is entitled to their own opinion, but they are not entitled to their own facts." My opinion is that the mind, matter and spirit entwine and merge into one. But each of us is the best judge of what we feel to be true for our inner self. I believe that spiritual practice is essential for personal well-being. Unless we understand and manage our own thoughts and emotions, we cannot be balanced, calm or happy.

Acquiring the knowledge about the truth of our existence, and knowing how to manage the incessant churning of our thoughts is essential to the art of living.

The realization of the truth within our inner self, is to me, the enlightenment I wish to achieve in my life, rather than devoting my time to praying, chanting or believing in some external mystical consciousness.

The *Mandukya Upanishad* says that 'enlightenment is a state of freedom from the ignorance that causes suffering. We may not attain belief in God, but it is essential to have the profound knowledge of the truth behind the concept of God. The idea is not to know God as a different being but as one's real self and essential nature, which is also the self of everything. Religion makes people dependent on priests, temples, idols, blind faith, and dogma. Such dependence is a habit of the lower mind. Such crutches are useful at a certain stage for some people, but they do not lead to the ultimate truth. A dependent mind is not free, and without freedom, enlightenment is impossible. Religious dogmas, beliefs and myths do not satisfy the human intellect while binding believers to a narrow view of life and human potential. Such preaching instils fear rather than love in the hearts of the masses.'

Thus, my endeavour throughout has been to seek the ultimate truth, hidden in all of us, irrespective of its source and to understand the meaning of that truth through experiential-realization, without blindly following any faith or dogma. Such a journey awakens in one the truth about the realities of life, where there are no more paradoxes, dualities or illusions of ego.

Yet, how freely we use the words truth, belief and faith, presuming we are aware of their import. What suits us becomes true? Actually, a belief is merely an opinion or conviction about what we think is true – which may or may not in fact be so. Faith is belief without evidence, which we blindly pursue as the truth. Knowledge is the information we gain through experience or from secondary sources. But that too has its limitations. We have no choice but to live by faith. What is important is what we base our faith on.

Knowing the truth is the most difficult thing for

the mind. In reality, truth can never be captured by the mind. As it receives and processes data, it changes from person to person. Truth can only be experienced in the now, as I shall elaborate in greater detail later. All of us are entitled to our own truth. For this very reason, spiritualism is based on living, experiencing and realizing the truth, rather than reading or hearing about it from someone else.

In worldly life, the mind plays games, hiding the truth from the Self. It gives numerous explanations, excuses, ifs and buts, denying the truth, especially when it hurts our self-interest. Knowing the self is the biggest truth. If we find the truth within, we have found God.

When we know the truth, it sets us free. Our behaviour changes for the better; the mind is no longer dependent on autosuggestions from the past or on nervous emotions. The mind is under our control and has the clarity necessary to affect the correct behaviour, leading us towards a natural flowering of our personality. Being true to oneself changes the way we are – our mannerisms, personality and our life.

Mind says: we are what we think.
Spirit says: we are when we do not think.
Mind says: life is in duality.
Spirit says: life is in oneness.
Mind says: I am the Knower.
Spirit says: knower and known are the same.
Mind says: God is our lord and almighty.
Spirit says: God and we are one.

Chapter 2
Body, Mind & Spirit

We all wish to live well; more than living long. How beautiful life would be if we could operate at full acceleration, irrespective of age or position in life; to be filled with energy and creative zeal; to have zest in our stride; to have feelings of love and peace in our hearts; to be supercharged with energy and feel completely alive and connected to life. A full and complete life is possible when we are concerned with what and how much we eat, how we listen to and care for the body, and how we balance the physical, emotional, mental and spiritual dimensions.

We know that beneath the layers of chemical activity, the body is just energy – an energy system with vibrating cells. Any disruption in this cellular energy causes disease. To maintain cellular equilibrium, there has to be a balance in the intake and output of energy.

There is no doubt that every single body cell is influenced by the way we think and feel. Our thoughts and emotions are stored in the vibration code and energy levels of our cells, and can thus alter or modify our biochemical profile. The mind is a powerful machine and asserts considerable control over the body. It can affect the body in many ways. The detrimental aspect is manifested when the mind is overpowered by negative thoughts like anxiety, depression, jealousy, hatred, etc.; thereby creating disease.

Today, science refutes the age-old theory that we are bound being victims of our genetic code. The Epigenetic Control claims that according to the exposure of our cellular level to the environment and with the spiritual intervention; thoughts, beliefs, attitudes and intention that we carry in our mind towards that environment alters the expression of the genetic code. The way we alter our self-consciousness through awareness by taking control over our mind. Similarly we can alter our genes to change their expressions of emitting the way we wish. Each cell has a consciousness, which changes in accordance to our given direction through our conviction, belief and its environment. Therefore, the secret of living is not determined by your genes but by your overall consciousness; within the mechanism of your starting form, within your mind going into every cell membrane, which collectively decide as a community and the surroundings of your living.

Our normal body activities such as breathing, digestion, sleeping, etc. are all controlled and cared for by the autonomous nervous system, with no inputs from us. We take our body for granted. We abuse it, telling it to shut up instead of listening to it, as we should. We take pride in boasting how much we can party or drink, or show off by saying that we sleep till noon. No wonder we need drugs to smother the weaknesses we have caused the body; it survives in spite of us, not because of us.

The mind and body interact and influence each other psychologically, physiologically and psychosomatically as expressions of each other. The state of the mind has a direct effect on us, while that of the body is indirect. If the body is unwell, it is difficult to be in a happy frame of mind. Unless we respect the body, we cannot coordinate the mind. Only by understanding the body with clarity and passion, can we balance the mind.

Therefore, even if your genetic map contains a cancer program, the same need not be expressed through the consciousness of your cell membrane unless your mind through its power of conviction agrees to it. Meaning, the switch 'on' and 'off' button is primarily dependent on your mind and its environment.

This reveals that you are a part of your environment in the way we think, exercise, eat, supplement, manage stress and sleep, social network, exposure to toxic substances; all and everything that you put into your body through all this, the mind determines the way your genes get the information to express themselves.

Now we come to the relationship of body-mind with the spirit – the center of consciousness, which I believe, is seated in our subconscious, and possesses infinite and unlimited energy. The sum total of body, mind and spirit forms our personality, uniqueness and individuality. The spirit plays a major role. In life, the physiological, psychological and spiritual play various parts. The body is navigated mainly by the mind, and the spirit drives the mind. The spirit reads our thoughts and witnesses the reasoning and meaning behind them. Thought would have been a mechanical process unless the spirit entered as the witnessing Self to challenge the mind about who, how, where and what is right or wrong.

Through this interpretation the mind is able to determine its own intentions and go forward.

What is the spirit? Besides being referred to as the subtle Witnessing Self, telling us we are not the body and mind but the spirit, it is the intelligent-energy which makes us think, act and interact in awareness. Awareness is the spiritual intelligence without which the mind cannot be conscious to experience and realize whatever we think.

When energy manifests in the mind, it takes the form of awareness, just as energy released from the sun takes the form of light. This awareness makes the mind aware of itself and its surroundings though consciousness. The content of the mind meets objects and turns into the duality of ego at one end and divine consciousness on the other. Divine consciousness is Pure consciousness, where no ego remains. This happens when consciousness merges with Total awareness as one. Then we achieve godhead – a rare form of absolute existence, reached only by a few.

Quantum theory concludes that a single energy is the source of everything. This energy is represented in different forms as nuclear, thermal, electrical, etc. Most scientists agree that for this energy to operate, it has to have a unified field of force such as gravity, electromechanical, electrochemical, nuclear, etc.

In the mental realm, only thoughts can be measured by science, as thoughts are mechanical. But here too, science is limited only to measuring the state before thoughts become conscious (i.e. the unconscious state). Science has not thrown any light upon the energy of our mental field and the intangible intelligence through which it acquires knowledge, experience and realization.

Einstein, who introduced the Theory of Relativity, was more concerned with the relationship between energy and matter; the meaning of consciousness and experience was left unexplored. It was David Bohm who claimed there was a unified energy and thought was distributed in various fields which did not follow other quantum entities in the conventional model of space and time. His Theory of Implicate Order covered a holistic view of 'the unbroken wholeness of the totality of existence as an undivided flowing movement without borders'.

Unable to confirm spirit or the unified field of consciousness as a defined mental energy, science refers to it as mystical spirit. Even today, scientists refer to consciousness as a by-product of electrochemical or neural activity within the mind. However, science has come very close to the spiritual connotation that all that exists in this universe is *Brahman,* referring to it as one energy. Until science proves reality to be conscience, existing as a unified field of energy, it will continue to refer to it as spirit.

No doctor can tell us when and what will happen to us, or how accurately his medicines are going to work. He can only tell us what the clinical or statistical picture looks like, and prescribe accordingly. The effect, as we are all aware, differs in every individual. Moreover, diseases such as cancer or allergies are not known to be overcome through the mere disposition of our minds. They create havoc with the immune system, and a series of reactions are triggered automatically.

Each one of us has to face the battle in our own unique way, being subject to unpredictable occurrences, irrespective of the desire to become well, mentally or by medicines. Here, the subconscious or the spirit plays its role, where the power of intention comes in. If we wish, we can command our subconscious to reprogram the software of the mind to change the printout of the body. That is why we come across cases that defy science, and in many cases, the incurable are cured and the credit is given to God. The famous, Dr Dean Ornish with his 35 years of research on preventing and reversing chronic diseases gives a lot of credit to spiritual techniques.

In our mind, there is a clear segregation between the conscious and the sub-conscious parts. The conscious part, they say, is hardly used by 5%, which has all your wants, wishes, desires, attachments, aspirations, etc. The sub-conscious, the storehouse of data as memory is the driving machine from where all the collective beliefs pour out. It plays back what has been conditioned or recorded over generations and is responsible in forming your consciousness, playing a major role in your determinism. Your whole personality revolves around your sub-conscious whether it is functioning out of conditioned blind beliefs by others or through your own reasoning in common sense.

Unless we respect all three dimensions in ourselves, we can never be integrated or balanced. This is where quantum healing comes in. For an ideal life, the body, mind and spirit have to be in perfect balance and this can only happen if we operate our body from the depths of our awareness. We need to remember that all three: body, mind and soul are interconnected as one. Each plays an important role because one cannot manifest or even exist without the other. It is only when all three are in consonance that your purpose in existence shall be fulfilled.

The energy field, which brings life into the body, need not die when it ceases to exist. Energy does not depend on oxygen or any other support system. The flow of energy needs to be enhanced to higher levels by proper breathing, diet, exercise, and mind management techniques, into a state of balance whereby it flows through the body unimpeded.

The question here is whether this intelligence-energy field, consciousness, or soul, moves and transfers when the body ceases to exist, into another state of being or afterlife. It is also said that we are reaching the age when we might share our lives with super intelligent chips without consciousness, implanted in our mind, dictating our lives. These chips, as declared by Dr Ray Kurzweil, are an evolutionary race between machine and human, embedded in our brains. They will eventually reverse ageing, thus prolonging our lifespan indefinitely. Until then, I suggest let us stick to balancing the mind and body with the spirit.

A full and complete life can be crafted when we are concerned with what and how much we eat, how we listen to and take care of our body, and how we handle ourselves in balancing the physical, emotional, mental and spiritual dimensions.

In Self-knowledge, we know what spirit is.
In Self-awareness, we are conscious of the spirit.
In Self-experience, we ignite the spirit.
In Self-realization,
We become one with that spirit.

Chapter 3
What is Spiritualism?
Part I

I wish to convey with all sincerity that there is nothing more worthy in life than knowing, living and realizing the essence of spiritualism. In spite of what we may attain in the form of knowledge, intellect, wealth, possessions or attachments, the search for the meaning and purpose of life can never be complete without Self-knowledge, Self-awareness and Self-realization. Only spiritualism, when compared to religion or science, is complete enough to provide these ultimate answers.

Spiritualism is neither a part of religion nor a science. For years it was restricted to being practiced in *ashrams* and monasteries. With the advent of new-age gurus, spiritualism has been made simpler – something each of us can understand, experience and practice. Science and technology are dynamic and have provided great opportunities for the progress of the outer world. Religion and its teachings, remain static. It is only the synthesis of all three – science, religion and spiritualism – that can create fulfilment and totality, whereby we can experience wealth, comfort, prayer, meditation and joy as one whole.

The wholeness and fullness of life, which we all desire – those attributes, both within and beyond, reveal the oneness of the material and spiritual worlds. While we constantly focus on our materialistic lives, we forget the other half – the divinity that resides within us.

Our energies become separated into good/bad, positive/negative, God/Devil – giving rise to conflicts of lust, jealousy, greed, etc. We remain enmeshed in delusions of materialism, wondering what is amiss: why is there such emptiness despite having so much?

The basic message of spiritualism purports to the power of nothingness, asserting that everything is but a form of spirit or energy, which encompasses both God and the Devil. Both God and we, are but manifestations of that same energy, where nothing is everything (explained in detail later), comprising all that exists in this Universe.

Spiritualism makes us aware that the body and mind exist only as ego; transcendence comes with awareness of the spirit which enlightens the powers of reasoning and common sense, helping us realize that consciousness can be raised, not by seeking or desiring, but through Self-knowledge – the experience and realization of who and what we are.

We are not required to search for enlightenment, *nirvana* or *moksha* in spiritualism, but to quiet the forever chattering mind with its outer, perceptual thoughts, wants and desires; countering them with spiritual ones. I am sure there are many who are eager to explore basic existential questions like: Who am I? Who is God? Where do we come from? What is life? What happens after death? What is my purpose in life? Science has been unable to give us complete answers; religion merely tells us to have faith and believe in God.

These books are based on such questions and existential factors. What follows is an in-depth study of our reality and truth, meant for those who wish to seriously study this subject. The focus is less on beliefs and dogmas and more on practical methods of self-development. There are many explanations contrary to received wisdom; where our powers of reasoning will determine what to believe and follow.

We start with the premise that spirit permeates, penetrates and prevails in all that there is in this universe, and that the core of this spirit is contingent upon the level of our spiritual awareness, in order for us to realize our true potential. Awareness is not a state of mind or a mental process, which keeps changing. It is luminous, absolute, non-dual energy – the light through which consciousness shines.

There can be no activity in the mind – thinking, feeling, memory, etc. – without the presence of this radiant energy. It is the same energy that reveals objective reality through our individual inner and outer perceptions, via experiences. It is beyond everything and any subject-object relationship, which the mind can conceive. The subject of awareness is discussed in great detail to define, clarify and contextualize this subject; simplify the difference between truth and falsehood with respect to the Creator and creation, as connected to our lives.

A truly realized master can explain this process, but such souls are rare, leaving us wondering whom to approach. Spiritualism, like other fields of human involvement today, is often perceived as a business, governed by a hankering for fame, acknowledgement and money; where the number of followers demonstrate strength.

For centuries, religion and politics have consoled the poor by promising them a beautiful afterlife; relying on the rich for their own sustenance, maintenance and prominence. Karl Marx aptly stated that, 'religion is the opium of the masses'. Politicians go a step further by telling the weak and poor that the rich are their enemies, responsible for taking away what little they have, while they are the ones who can provide what is needed. Many spiritual gurus too, take advantage of the situation by increasing the number of blind-faith followers; proclaiming that our sufferings are due to our past *karma,* insinuating that since we have attained human birth, the future shall be bright – thereby providing temporary psychological relief.

At the time of the origins of spiritualism, over 5000 years ago, when the *Upanishad*s were first documented, our learned seers and sages had affluent or royal patrons. The beneficiaries first provided food, clothing and shelter for their families and themselves, only then did they devote themselves to self-actualization or spiritualism and the exploration of such abstract questions as: 'Who am I?' and 'What is my purpose in life?'

The poor could barely manage to fulfil their minimal needs, with their desires and needs remaining unfulfilled. What can spiritualism provide in such cases, except the promise of a better future and consolation through faith, belief and dogmas? No religious or political precepts, even today, are concerned about the needy, except in providing temporary relief through charity and aid, telling them to continue following their faith. The aid too, often has strings attached.

The study of spiritualism is for those whose basic needs have been satisfied. The reason being, that when physical needs have been met, the need for something beyond arises. It is only after reaching this stage of life that we start considering methods of meditation, yoga, awareness, consciousness, oneness, ultimate reality, etc. Incessant thoughts of jealousy, lust, greed and desire followed by anxiety, despair and depression propel us forward, providing that fodder in understanding what the mind actually wants.

Spiritualism started in India as a luxurious way of living. The ancient scriptures, going back over 5000 years, were called the *Vedas*, from which the philosophical *Upanishads* arose. These scriptures are as relevant today as they were then. It was a period when India basked in its riches, before invaders – from the Mongol Genghis Khan, the Greek Alexander, the Afghani Mughals, the Portuguese, French and British – arrived to ransack the country and leave it in poverty.

The four prime requisites for a fulfilling life, as given in the *Vedas*, are: achieving economic progress through righteousness in order to accomplish one's desires and thus take the path towards *moksha* or liberation.

Spiritualism is based on the ideal of the totality and wholeness of life. There are three levels of existence; physical considered to be illusory, empirical, the stage where cause and effect are perceived through experience and the absolute, the stage which awakens the mind towards the spirit, ultimately leading you towards that final goal, where the mind and body dissolve as One liberating itself into *moksha*.

Both the illusory and the empirical are as real as the absolute, because in each we have the absolute besides the relative as the content. While the existence of living in illusions with desire and attachments appear and disappear, the empirical leads us towards that experiential living where we come to understand the spirit both as an individual soul in ego and also as the ultimate in the form of the Witnessing Self residing within us.

The absolute existence is more of a vision, for such enlightenment or Self-realization is a rare achievement in human form.

Moreover, Self-realization is more in experiencing and realizing than seeking. Lord Buddha never sought enlightenment, he simply realized the same through his experiences. It can be achieved through the practice of *karma-yoga* (selflessness) and *bhakti-yoga* (devotion, compassion and non-attachment). We should aim for non-attachment rather than detachment, because detaching involves unfastening something after it has already been bound.

One should note here that if sensuous desires remain unfulfilled or suppressed, it might be harmful for an individual. Such negative energy could emerge later to trouble us with greater force. Once such desires are fulfilled, only then should we consider the dimensions beyond our immediate existence, and venture into that realm of consciousness that our witnessing self wishes us to conquer.

We read and hear that we should go within, into the inner world, to seek spiritual enlightenment. The meaning of that lies in the fact that inner practice is entirely based on experiential living rather than learning. Experiences are always intrinsic and specific to the individual.

Our existence, in spite of worldly wealth and comforts, remains incomplete. This emptiness can only be assuaged by spiritual means. Neither religion nor science has been successful in filling this void. Only spiritualism, which aims to nullify the chattering of our thoughts and the mind ruling us through emotions, has been able to give us satisfactory answers to our ever-growing wants and attachments. It teaches us how to quiet the mind through methods, which allows us to use the mind, rather than be used by it.

Spiritualism is not a luxury anymore; it has become a necessity today, in the midst of chaos and an egotistical mode of living, based on the credo of 'I, Me, My, Mine, and Myself'. We need to absorb the depth of the concepts within the simple meanings of 'inter-relationship', 'inter-connectedness' and 'inter-dependence', which are important precepts in spiritualism. Instead, in the world today, we see more of separatism, individualism and materialism. We push, strangle, crush and kill one another in the name of religion, power and money.

We have to understand the message behind spiritual realization – that what we perceive, think and feel is not who we are. By becoming aware of our deeper, conscious self, we become aware that we are not just body and mind; but we are the Witnessing Self that observes and makes us aware of all that we perceive through our thoughts and sensory organs.

The next three chapters explain spiritualism in

detail. Spiritualism primarily teaches us to know our real Self, freeing us from ignorance and the illusions that the mind forms through external perceptions. In the study of spiritualism, we learn about an inner transformation, which has no connection with any religion. Religion believes in separate gods; spiritualism sees each of us as a part of God.

We need to awaken to that spiritual experience and realize the inner self, in spontaneous awareness, in order to become conscious of our inner and outer perceptions. We are far more than the limitations of our perception of desires; attachments and sentiments allow us to experience. The essence of spiritualism lies in living in awareness, from one moment to the next, in mindfulness and consciousness of who and what we are.

The mind is designed for self-interest in selfish desires – the reason for so much stress and many ailments. Further, the mind interprets the world through thoughts and words, which are connected to the past or project into the future. The mind can never capture the now. In the time taken for thoughts to receive inputs from the sensory organs, analyze and transmit them, a new 'now' arrives and replaces the old.

The mind can, at most, experience the now. It is spiritualism, which teaches the mind how to be open to the presence of the now and the presence of all that exists in the awareness of now. Therefore, a complete interconnection of the past, present and future is the essence of spiritualism. It is that process of living where we are more concerned with purpose, fulfilment and completeness of life rather than realizing enlightenment.

Spiritual gurus often stray away from the real teachings of spiritualism for the sake of recognition, fame, money and requiring funds for maintaining their organizations. They dazzle their followers by preaching high ideals of Self-realization in pure consciousness, which is neither possible nor meant for average mortals. We should keep in mind that if any 'Guru' is blessed with mystical powers or *siddhis*, these are generally not displayed, promoted, marketed or sold.

'Pure consciousness'; 'Self-realization'; 'I am That,' are high-flown words about the supreme reality. They are correct in their own place but are also far too visionary for us. These concepts are meant for knowing God rather than to promote self-development. The net result is that, even after listening to such discourses, disciples remain in the same rut of ego and body-consciousness while talking proudly about their newly acquired knowledge of spiritualism.

What we need to know and remember is that the rise in consciousness/awareness is the consequence of the energy field attracting itself closer to the oneness of its own experiential self, rather than the result of human volition. Just 'be', rather than 'become' in desire.

Awareness is above intellect and intellect above thought,
Thought is above the senses, but above all, deep within,
Is that unconditioned I am,
where mortal becomes immortal.

Part II

The fundamental teachings of spiritualism enforce a sense of oneness, interconnectedness and interdependence with all that exists in our Universe, expounding that no 'one' can exist without the 'other'. What better, non-physical, alternate healing precept can we hope for to calm and change the chaos and isolation we live in?

Healing the mind by inculcating thoughts of acceptance of all good and bad in meditative awareness improves health by effecting higher levels of calm and improved longevity. It also fosters a society based on truth, morality and virtues, leading to peace and co-operation and unification, rather than separateness.

Essentially, both religion and spiritualism seek love, compassion and togetherness. In the final stages, both merge into one, in unity. However, religion today often preaches insularity and a sense of being separate; while spiritualism demands oneness through self-discovery. Whether we choose both or either, is for us to decide. In religion, we are taught to believe in the God provided to us by birth and community; in spiritualism, we find divinity within our self and in all beings as One.

Today, religion and spiritualism are being confused in the name of God. Many spiritual gurus, instead of relaying spiritualism's simplicity, are mixing the two. People continue to follow blindly as devotees and continue to live in the same separateness, academically 'knowing' the supreme knowledge but minus its experience.

The goal of a guru's teaching, in ancient times, was to convert a student into a master. But today, we have become blind followers. Hence, we remain ignorant. Disciples prefer to speak of the various experiences of their gurus in ego-consciousness, rather than practising the realistic spiritual methods meant for us. Attaining super-consciousness and God-realization on a paranormal basis is not the answer. We need to be experientially sound, depending on our own capacity and physical reality; by choosing methods suited to our own level of development.

We are responsible, for the level of our own consciousness, which might differ entirely from what someone else – a guru for instance, might achieve or deliver as an ideal. Remember, that awareness may just be the context in determining 'who we are'; but today, we are not who we will be tomorrow, for that depends on the spiritual evolution we experience from one moment to the next.

In fact, it is extremely important to have a guru for self-development in practising spiritual upliftment. By following only our own theories, we may easily become the victims of pride and ego, with the weaknesses and delusions of materialistic life remaining within. When we follow a guru, we do so in humility, and gain a deeper understanding of the divine reality within. However, since a true guru is rare, and since it is difficult to discern who a realized guru is, we are usually left with no choice but to self-develop in order to self-experience and realize the fundamental truths of existence. Blessed are the few who actually find a true guru.

I feel, what we need today is more of collective common sense, intuitive realism and reasoning in daily life, rather than pundits and preachers telling us in their religious style, how to live a balanced life encompassing both worldly and spiritual domains. If spiritualism were to take religion over, the world would be a much happier place, with higher morals, compassion and ethical values in awareness.

What needs to be emphasized here is that spiritualism contains those proper answers on how to exist and lead one's life – as long as we understand its relevance and experience to realize those methods as provided later, of living in a fruitful manner, from the right source.

Even though most scientists shy away from accepting what the mystics have declared, we do notice a gradual reconciliation between scientific theory and the truths long declared by ancient seers. Let us consider some salient features.

Spiritualism declares:

1. Existence in body and mind is an illusion (*maya*), which is apparent and changeable, and limited to space and time. *Brahman* or spirit is the eternal reality, existing in limitless, spaceless, timeless awareness.

- Science has accepted this more or less as a fact, claiming that existence is merely an optical illusion; we exist as a condensed form of organized energy, which keeps changing from one form of reality to another.

2. *Brahman* or spirit is all that exists in the universe. This essential creation is one and not two.

- ➢ Even this has now been scientifically agreed upon – all that exists is energy, which can neither be created nor destroyed; regardless of changes, it remains constant as a single entity comprising of multiple fields, but in different forms, shapes and sizes.

3. In spiritualism, nothingness represents *shunya* or zero, which does not signify emptiness or nothingness, but everything. It is not merely a placeholder but the indestructible centre between positive and negative numbers connected to infinity.

   - ➢ Science now considers 'nothing' as not empty but filled with something that came before the beginning of nothing. The universe is filled with space in the form of dark energy and comprises a net infinite energy of zero. Even in a vacuum, as confirmed by physicist, Hendrik Casimir, a measurable force exists in the absence of any known field.

4. In the *Vedas* it has been said that for material reality to exist, we must have a conscious reality, which is

connected, to a unified field of consciousness known as the Ultimate Reality.

- Science, as of now, has no answer to how experience emerges or the mind becomes aware and conscious of physical and mental reality.

This provides a glimpse into the depth behind spiritualism. We shall discover more about how it defines the Ultimate Reality as we read on. Spiritualism, in fact, is a link between the external and internal necessities of humanity. Both are to be embraced in totality and oneness, and practiced in balance and moderation, not through impractical high ideals probably suited only to a few.

Therefore, remove the mask. First and foremost, learn the difficult thing – knowing oneself or being true to our own self. Be fulfilled externally and then venture into the realm of spiritualism to learn about witnessing the self, about expanding the consciousness, and how to undertake the journey of awakening from ignorance to enter the inner world of spiritual awareness.

Spiritualism is not something we can seek and

attain. The Buddha did not seek any enlightenment, nor did he follow any religion. He realized enlightenment through mindfulness; by meditating from one moment to the next in the presence of the now.

Transcendental meditation works more as therapy to give temporary relief to the body, mind and soul. Spiritual meditation is living within that presence, from one moment to the next in awareness – accepting, indulging, experiencing, outgrowing, transforming and realizing the oneness of what we already are. All this will be elaborated in greater detail later.

The need for spiritual living arises from the fact that normal existence is based on the principle of dualities. The mind cannot survive without separating the world into opposites. If there is profit, there will also be loss, if there is a plus, we need a minus to balance the two. In the vicious cycle of living in this manner, there comes a stage when we realize there has to be something more to life than simply eating, drinking and making money.

Unlike science, spiritualism is concerned about knowing and living with the subject, in observance and alertness, in spontaneity, with awareness, in the presence of the now. This study goes beyond sensory inputs to the subject of consciousness.

There are four aspects one needs to follow: first, knowing oneself in honesty, without any judgment; second, knowing the subtle, Witnessing Self, which exists beyond our thoughts and emotions; third, experiencing and realizing the power of the now, through meditation and with awareness in every moment; and fourth, experiencing God through compassion, selflessness and non-attachment.

In external perception, there are four factors which determine any experience: the object in question, the sense-organ, the mind, and the conscious self. The mind connects the perceived object to the subject of who we are – the knowing self. Therefore, knowledge is the manifestation of the knowing self, connected through the mind, to experience, forming our consciousness and external perception, to determine anything. The study of inner perception of consciousness or spirit, is spiritualism.

Spiritualism emphasizes on three modes of existence:

1. Illusory or perceptive existence, where objects appear and disappear.

2. Empirical existence, where inner perception deals with cause and effect through experiences.

3. Absolute existence, when the body and mind dissolve into unified consciousness, in the absence of any inner or outer perception; defying all the laws of mind, ego and desire, to become absolute or Pure Consciousness in Self-Realization (as achieved by a few, like the Buddha, Jesus, Krishna, etc.).

Conscience is not a characteristic of the mind but the essence of the self. It is only through this intelligent-energy that awareness illuminates consciousness to manifest in the mind. The mind, under normal circumstances, is consumed in its own body- ego-consciousness, until spontaneous awareness creates that elusive inner perception, making mind aware of its own true reality.

This makes the mind conscious of its doings; it becomes aware of the Witnessing Self. Therefore, we are not just the body and mind, but also the awareness, which foresees the emergence of conscience to direct the mind through all its experiences. It is preeminent in everything the mind indulges in; making the mind aware and conscious of its thoughts and actions.

In spiritualism, awareness is the absolute spiritual energy, which transforms intellect and reason into a higher level of consciousness. In this manner, one reveals both ignorance and knowledge through a series of experiences, forming one's consciousness from the awareness realized.

In receiving awareness, the mind becomes capable of knowing what it knows. External perception involves the mind, choosing and discriminating; in experiencing opposites or dualities – leading to conflicts, anxiety and despair. It is awareness, which balances those dualities by bringing us closer to the oneness of the energy we are all made of. This is the role spiritualism plays, revealing the nature and composition of who we really are.

The problem with perceptual thinking by the senses is that it releases concentrated mental and physical energy with properties of disintegration, depending on the level of desire, ego, emotional attachment and self-centeredness. Due to this disintegrative power, the mind separates the psychic energy into opposites, in order to choose the aspect favourable to us. This phenomenon also exists in materialistic living, where self-interest is the primary factor; but this damages the body, mind and soul, as it eventually leads to conflicts, anxiety and suffering.

In order to achieve balance, we can turn to intuitive thinking – the spontaneity of the now in awareness – where unlike sensuous perceptual thoughts we are proactive, spontaneous, observant and alert. The external perceptive mind is incomplete since it relates to thoughts of the past and future, extracting information from what it already knows. The intuitive mind, through observation and alertness, captures fresh awareness. We are in the presence of what we are doing, before thoughts of objectivity take over. This way, the mind releases the energies of immediate creativity, intuition, imagination and awareness.

The mind is mainly thought, and thinks primarily on our behalf and our ego, through the sense organs. The mind is designed for the body and its environment. But the same limited mind also has the capacity to manifest awareness, and to observe, experience and realize the infinite spirit.

All our progress or even our disasters occur through thought. Science too, is primarily dependent on thought, and for this reason it can operate only in the realm of objectivity. Spiritualism attempts to go beyond, into the subject of life, to the essence of experiential realization, where we can discover self-surrender, love and compassion for all, and the oneness, which we really are.

Thoughts have two directions in their functioning. The first is perception through the five senses, or collecting data. The second is intuition, the source of awareness and imagination, to make us aware and conscious, functioning as a witness in order to guide the mind between this and that. The first relies on past and future data, whereas the latter, helps us become absorbed in the presence of the now.

Perceptual thinking is designed for survival – where fear is the prime emotion. In intuitive thinking, love is the prime essence. Sensory perception, in order to exist, creates dualities in the mind and separates everything into two extremes. This part of the mind can only relate and function in duality, which is driven by ego.

The inner perception of the aware mind – depending on its level of consciousness – balances ego and duality through the power of acceptance and transformation. From these perceptions we develop our personality, uniqueness and individuality, which make us what we are.

In this manner, the mind experiences any object on three levels: a. physical, through perception; b. mental, through psychological experience;

and c. spiritual, through being in the presence of the moment. Here the experiencer (our aware consciousness), in experiencing (through the mind), the experienced (the object), represents the whole.

The conscience (the inner sense) which witnesses, observes, or experiences an event through the perceptive mind, cannot see or feel except through the objective sensory organs. Pure Consciousness is not an object, which can be seen. It is the witnessing subject in totality, the thinker. It is invisible, without gender, and can never be known, because it is the Knower. This intelligence-energy is part of universal consciousness in the form of the Witnessing Self in awareness. In this way, the mind connects to other minds and is in constant communication with the whole world.

Science is completely dependent on the sensory perceptive mind. It needs an object to perceive, observe, experiment and infer upon. It survives on theories of reductionism, randomness and natural selection; cutting, dissecting and analysing every form into its parts to study and infer what it perceives as scientific or true.

In spiritualism, truth is the presence, which can only be experienced. The oceans or the sun, exist permanently, but in their presence, waves and reflections vary, becoming the past or future. By the time the mind experiences truth and interprets the same, it gets distorted and merges into past experience, to reflect the future.

This is probably why science has been unable to understand the concept of consciousness. Spiritualism, on the other hand, considers collective or universal consciousness as its very basis.

I am the subject, I am the presence,
and I am that being who is aware.
I am that limitless, non-dual awareness separated into a subject-object relationship.

Part III

Spiritualism claims that everything is just a manifestation of the One, and it is this collective consciousness, which forms a network to bind everything together. But the external mind is the very opposite, breaking every fundamental rule of nature through self-interest and self-centeredness, separating everything into dualities.

The three main attributes of spiritualism are:

1. Everything that exists in this universe is but the manifestation of the One.

2. The existence of the body and mind is just an illusion. The essence of life lies in the total awareness of who and what we are.
3. Consciousness arises with individual awareness and transmigrates from one body to another in cycles of birth and death; to finally reunite with the one undivided universal consciousness referred to as spirit.

Spiritualism calms the mind, which is forever in wanting mode, going from one desire to another. It means going beyond the body and mind to the spirit – where there is compassion and equanimity, selfless devotion to mankind and sensitivity to all, not just toward oneself. Spiritualism is not a myth. It has to be practiced through experience and realization, in daily life, rather than be learnt.

In spiritualism, awareness is the context from which conscience evolves. Consciousness is the sense of being or the presence of 'I am'. The ultimate goal should be to go beyond the duality of consciousness and unconsciousness. We must understand we are a part of the Absolute, which is pure and pristine awareness.

Consciousness is always related to an object for us to become conscious of it, but awareness is unaware till it manifests in the mind; it is never related to anything, not being dual but absolute. It is only when one Self-Realizes, through Pure Consciousness, and becomes one with the Absolute that total awareness is experienced.

Therefore, consciousness is part of the awareness within us, which we need in order to evolve and realize who we really are – body and mind or consciousness in awareness? The nature of consciousness may differ in waking, sleeping and dreaming states, but non-dual awareness remains the same at all times.

The maxim, 'Thou Art That' means, individual consciousness is none other than universal consciousness. It defines the relationship between God and us, stating that the Creator is none other than the creation. Therefore, the objective human form, mind and body, possesses the capacity to take our impure or separated consciousness back towards completeness through total awareness into Pure Consciousness, referred to as God.

Therefore, in spiritualism, 'I am that' or I am God, stands for – 'I am the same constituent as God, as a part of the same quality, which reaches totality only when self-consciousness becomes pure'. To be able to reach this pure state is extremely rare. When it happens, the body and mind dissolve and discard individual consciousness to merge into universal consciousness in Self-realization.

In spiritualism it is important to understand the meaning behind 'Thou art That' or 'I am That'. To do so, we must first understand that the body and mind are illusions of convertible energy and mass and all that I see, think and do with my sense organs, is subject to constant change. Hence I am neither 'this' nor 'that', both of which are temporary and can be considered observable reality only. So, what am 'I'?

Once these layers of electrochemistry – these optical illusions of mind and sensuous perceptual thoughts are taken away, what is left is the reality of my presence and consciousness through awareness. So, from gross energy of the body, I travel to the subtle, that is the mind, and then I remove those layers as well, and explore the core. What is left is only awareness.

As mentioned earlier, we can never capture the presence of the now because by the time the mind captures the now, a new now has taken its place. We can only *experience* the now, in the same manner that the understanding of who 'I Am' takes us to the reality that our conscience too, is dependent on the presence of cosmic energy – awareness.

Our comprehension of 'I Am' then gets connected to the universal presence of energy, becoming a part of all that exists, as one unified consciousness. This is the meaning and knowledge of God or 'I Am That' – that we are part of the same quality we know as God, but separated by dualities in order to exist in living form. Hence, I repeat, the Creator is none other than the creation. This truth, in totality can only be Self-realized by us in a state of *moksha,* in total awareness, in Pure Consciousness, when we dissolve the body and mind into the universal spirit or energy.

The nothingness we keep reading and speaking about, is in fact, everything – filled with indestructible, indivisible, absolute energy through awareness. We get separated from this absolute energy or spirit and become matter (body, mind and soul), to finally decompose and return to that same nothingness or energy.

One who wishes to live a spiritual life need not run away from the material – existential life. He must clearly understand the meaning of both worldly and spiritual life, and simultaneously live with awareness, in oneness; accepting, outgrowing and transforming his consciousness though awareness, to bring him closer to the reality of who he really is.

Given below are the salient features of worldly and spiritual living:

Worldly Living

- We exist as body and mind.
- Our five senses provide data, where the mind perceives, through its individual physical experience of factors like colour and sound.

- The perceptive mind is designed exclusively to live for its wants through desires, attachments and ego.
- The external mind lives in the dualities and vicious cycle of pleasure and pain. The mind discriminates and chooses what is better for itself.
- The external mind works solely for the benefit of the individual self, at the cost of everything else around.

Spiritual Living

- Intuition, imagination and creativity, from fresh intelligence-energy, enter the mind to manifest as immediate or spontaneous awareness.
- The spiritual mind channels true awareness to make the individual conscious of what he perceives and indulges in, which enables one to balance dualities and separateness.
- The spiritual mind thrives on non-duality and oneness while existing in a field of unified consciousness, in total awareness.
- The spiritual mind, after knowing the subject/ object relation, can experience and realize it

through awareness, thus accepting the existence in totality, outgrowing and transforming through an attitude of togetherness; moving towards the oneness that is one's real destination. This provides one with peace and fulfilment instead of separating everything into dualities for one's self-interest.

Spiritual living righteously in worldly living of materialism and desires must be merged in the right balance through an attitude of selfless devotion to oneness. This should be our purpose in life. We need to make that our worldview and live accordingly, to fulfil both, while keeping our focus on ultimately achieving unity with the Pure consciousness of our spirit.

Religion is based on belief.
Philosophy rationalizes belief.
Science is open to both, for or against belief.
Spiritualism superposes belief in awareness.

Chapter 4
Science, Religion & Spirituality
Part I

Today, man and science, after doing much damage to nature and the environment, are becoming aware about protecting Planet Earth, which has nourished man for generations over the millennia. We are realizing that besides the externalities of life, we also need to be spiritually aware – not because we love Mother Earth or Mankind, but because our very survival is at stake. Collective consciousness still remains a dream. As long as we continue to cut, divide, separate, excessively consume and waste our natural resources, we are doomed to suffer, disintegrate and vanish one day.

Man needs science and technological progress for evolution in the material world. Religion is needed for faith and identity. Faith is often fear-based, where one worries whether one goes to heaven or hell. The spiritual aspect of religion has been lost. Religion has turned into dogma, traditions, superstitions and myths, or the business of enrolling followers.

We do not fight wars or win elections based on spiritualism, as we often do with religion, politics and technology. Spiritualism is the experience of the inner 'us', bridging the gap between the unconscious and conscious. It is meant to propagate love, peace, harmony and joyous living. Spirituality is the experience of our individuality through consciousness. However, spiritualism has become an esoteric subject for study and discussion, rather than normal practice in actual living today.

Just as science is now aware of the oneness of energy through its study of fusion rather than fission (splitting), we too, need to awaken our consciousness and shed our ignorance about spirituality. We need to realize the interrelation, inter-connectedness and interdependence of all things and make that very realization the underlying metaphor for peaceful survival.

Spiritualism is a different subject from religion and science, even though the purpose of all three is to benefit mankind. Religion purports to be the path to a better existence, with its own terms, conditions and dogmas. Spiritualism, on the other hand, believes in the total surrender of the self, and acceptance of everything as one. It encompasses the whole of life in totality.

Spiritualism does not force upon you the choice of dualities; we need to have both worlds to live in wholesomeness – both material and spiritual living. We have a material mind in a material body, and we have the soul to balance them. There may be certain differences in the ideologies presented by various spiritual gurus but even if their paths differ, their purpose leads to the same realization – that ultimately we are all one. The absolute content in both good and bad are the same, it is the mind which separates the Absolute into dualities.

Some religions separate one God from another. Science, of course, has no belief in God or anything else, unless proven. Science is about materialism and external development of personalities, leading to ego. Greater the luxuries, proportionately is the increase in the separatist attitude of the ego. Science, of course has no definition or understanding of morality.

Legend and folk tales with supernatural heroes and sacred incidents became intertwined with religious beliefs. Religion, in a broader sense, brings together mythology, theology, spiritualism, rituals, morality, etc. In ancient times, seers and sages found it easier to explain and elaborate upon difficult concepts of spiritualism, using mystical stories. These stories also became a convenient way to communicate and arouse interest in the minds of common people about the subtle truths and messages of spiritualism.

Even today, the most bizarre stories are accepted as religious truth and believed. This has laid the ground for superstition and dogma to flourish. Rationality has disappeared and the sublime message of togetherness and oneness has turned into separations – separate gods for separate beliefs.

Spiritualism and religion, first originated in India and then travelled to China, Greece and Arabia. Even though Hinduism, being more of a philosophy and way of living, is also considered as the first known religion. Hinduism is closest to spiritualism even today, and one can pray to anything or anybody, with total acceptance, respect and freedom for every other religion. While Hindus do convert to other religions, there is no concept of converting to Hinduism, because of its core belief in the oneness of all.

Hinduism, in the days of yore, spread far and wide. Today, the ruins at Angkor Vat depicting from Hindu mythology in Cambodia and ancient Hindu temples exist in Indonesia. Ironically, due to its acceptance of all religions, instead of becoming stronger, Hinduism has become confined mainly to India and Nepal, demonstrating how separation rules over oneness in worldly life.

Whether Eastern or Western, this religion or that, it is time to realize that wealth and fame on their own are bound to lead to problems – if spiritualism is not taken seriously, to balance, silence, and control the forever-demanding mind. Spiritualism is in fact, a link between the external and internal necessities of mankind. Both should be embraced in totality and oneness; and practiced in balance and moderation.

Both religion and spiritualism have not been able to succeed in the purpose for which they were designed. The rich pray for peace and tranquillity, to eliminate fear and insecurity; the rest demand something or the other according to their needs or wants. No one is interested in knowing the real essence of spiritualism and its aim of awakening the spirit lying dormant within us. Spirituality is all about living in observance, being alert; accepting all situations in awareness; to transform and attain the fullness that life has to offer; conquering the brooding and constant chattering of the mind.

Science needs proof.
Religion requires faith.
Spiritualism demands unconditional love.
Eventually, they all merge into the One.

Part II

Science is still pondering how atoms, protons, and over a hundred billion neurons in the brain create the power to think, experience and realize. What also intrigues scientists is how the mind is so aware in the realm of consciousness. Does the brain, which is material, has mass and is composed of matter, have a link to an invisible psychic energy field?

Science and the mind, functioning with the aid of sensory organs, have their limitations as they can only study what can be observed in objective form. Conscience thus remains a mystery to science and we have to turn to philosophers and spiritualists who declare it to be everything, for fulfilment and enlightenment; but it can only be experienced or internally perceived. They refer to it as the eternal essence of life.

Spiritualism declares – conscience or the inner sense is not mystical, but the very subject of life, where existence takes place as the object. It states that awareness is the ultimate subjective psychic energy, indestructible and indivisible in the human mind, superseding perceptive thought. However, to prove this is not the aim of spiritualism. On one hand, we have Pure Consciousness or total awareness – when one reaches a state of bliss. On the other hand, there is physical existence, where we remain locked in a vicious cycle of pleasure and pain.

Spirituality essentially means the spirit or the degree of awareness, which manifests as self-awareness within us, forming our individuality. It is this witnessing force, which arises from the field of unified consciousness and is responsible for balancing our inner perceptions with the external ones received from our sensory organs.

The *Upanishads* divided the whole domain of spirituality into four, thousands of years before any formal religion existed:

- Reality is permanent and changeless. It exists, encompassing everything, manifesting as part of a complete whole. You may refer to this as spirit, energy, soul or consciousness, which cannot be created nor destroyed.
- The spirit, in manifesting through the mind, becomes aware and conscious of what one is about to experience.
- This awareness and individual consciousness reveals our ignorance. Otherwise, the mind remains in a state of illusion or *maya*, till it reaches its final destination of oneness, from which it has been separated by duality.
- Conscience in every human is a part of the

> total grid of consciousness in continuum; remaining as intelligence–energy in the form of spirit, transmigrating from one cycle of birth and death to another.

Spiritualism in those ancient days, spread from one civilization to another, from one continent to another. Enlightened ones like the Buddha and Jesus based their teachings on its foundations, making changes according to their own understanding and awareness. They offered a higher reality to their followers than was the current perception – an existing parallel to perceived reality, through awareness. This higher reality enhanced a person's individuality, awakening him to the spirit of consciousness, through awareness, to gain knowledge about his real Self.

Science, on the other hand, continues to rely on external perception; that too, based only on what can be observed of external reality, making the whole subject objectively oriented. Viewed through scientific eyes, the mind is that part of the brain which electro-chemically decides what we feel and genetically determines how we evolve and electro-magnetically functions in all its neural processes. For example, science can only believe in the truth and love which can be proven objectively. However, truth and love, like reality, need to be experienced, because what we externally perceive is constantly changing and that makes it unreal. Truth and love are subjective fields and they need to be experienced and realized, which is the nature of the substratum to which they belong.

Sensory thinking creates the illusion that something is real when it is only apparently real. A gold ornament is considered to be real, but it can be changed into something else. Light passing through a green glass appears green; trees seem to move in the opposite direction to a moving train.

Illusions disappear when the perception of the exact nature of the substratum is revealed; we then experience the illusion without delusion. Illusions also occur in differing ways within the workings of memory, dreams or hallucinations. Today, both science and spiritualism broadly accept perceptive illusion as temporary. The way a design can be superimposed on gold; similarly the 'I', as body and mind, is superimposed on the real Self through layers of flesh and our neural networks. We remain conscious and aware as the eternal Witnessing Self, even though being encased in that gross sheath.

Historically, religion has ruled supreme; but logic and science are gradually uprooting the base of blind faith. To the educated mind, it is fast losing its essence, being ineffective in solving any of the basic psychic problems of mankind. Spiritual doctrine, as laid down by seers millennia ago, expounded not only upon belief or faith, but also what a force and reality, the spirit is all about. Science is open to any faith as long as the facts are provided. Religion, on the other hand, is based on dogmas and beliefs leading to blind faith. Spiritualism simply declares the truth – that everything is the manifestation of the One.

Eventually, spiritualism is bound to flourish because of its message of oneness, togetherness and unification of all energies as science, religion and mankind learn to embrace it.

Science, despite its achievements and triumphs, remains confused on the subject of morality. This has led to the further separation and destruction of man and nature, rather than to humility and unity, paving a dangerous road for mankind. For example, the reality behind consciousness is experience, which science does not have any tools and instruments to measure and observe. It relies on theories of reductionism, which cannot be applied to consciousness.

Objective reality gradually disintegrates, whereas subjective reality, in the form of consciousness, keeps evolving in search of fulfilment in unification, oneness and completeness. Consciousness, manifesting in the mind, is designed for the ultimate role of becoming the Self. But, it exhibits itself as ego, giving the false impression of 'I' being the body and mind, in ego consciousness.

In this manner, the process of the evolution of consciousness continues until it reaches the final stage – total awareness in Pure Consciousness, when the individual self merges with the unified Self in a state of godliness. This stage, though extremely rare, if realized, is deemed to bestow supernatural powers upon the realized one.

Science can improve our lifestyle through material comforts, but when it comes to understanding consciousness, it still has a long way to go. Science and spiritualism are both essential, one for the physical realm and the other for the empirical. They are both relevant in their own domains; science by understanding the complexities of existence by reductionism in randomness; and spiritualism by understanding life as the practice of oneness.

This is the reason, when quantum physicists started studying the real composition of the body and mind; many of them were inspired by the spiritual declaration of Brahma, and finally came to the same conclusion – that everything that exists in our universe is a manifestation of energy. Scientific processes are based on hypothesis, research and experimentation; the inferences thus drawn are considered to be the truth. But the same inferences are liable to change with time and space, as knowledge advances. Science is versatile; it is open to change according to new research.

Spiritualism is based on principles of non-duality. *Advaita,* based on this philosophy, remains the same today. The truth of spiritualism never changes, for it has no relevance to space and time. It is an absolute experience of the now, which is eternal, existing in the presence of our being. But, when connected to the mind, it separates in each individual, into duality.

Science speaks about existence as related to the body and mind, in accordance with the past, present and future. Spiritualism refers to the presence of each moment, where life is a presence, a reality of the now, where the past, present and future merge in subjective changes, forming experiences. Truth and love are subjective experiences, which happen in the now, and are purely experiential; they can only be felt; they cannot be described in their entirety or essence by the mind.

Truth in spiritualism remains eternal, whereas scientific truths keep changing according to research. Science regards new inferences as new truths, relying on human intelligence. Spiritualism lives in consciousness.

Without science we would be nowhere. There is no doubt about its importance. But science is connected to thought processes through perception, and is therefore limited. It needs to go beyond to understand the complexity of how energy behaves in the human mind as a series of experiences called consciousness, and how this is linked to a unified consciousness – the One. Hence science and spiritualism complement the other to give us a more complete understanding of existence and Life.

Besides its usual methodology of cutting, dissecting and analysing, science keeps delving into unifying all that has been separated, by using objectivity. Spiritualism deals with the subject of a higher reality where God is an inward study instead of a separate God for every religion. Religion asks for blind faith and fear of God rather than love. Science, however, is open and clear, it is neither for nor against any faith. It only requires evidence.

Scientific progress has changed our world. But, let us ask ourselves: are we really happy? Mental unrest to mass destruction are as rampant today as they were during barbaric times; man has everything and yet nothing. He is still a slave to his incessant desires.

Spiritualism neutralizes and soothes us by clarifying truth and reality. The answer it provides is the path of selfless love and acceptance. If knowledge is the ultimate aim of science; then living, experiencing and realizing, is ultimate to spiritualism.

In spiritual living, channelling the knowledge of higher reality by practicing selfless love and awareness of oneness is considered the key. We thus respect one another and accept every situation, moment by moment, as it unfolds; realizing our true presence not only as body and mind, but as core energy, which is soul and spirit; aware and complete in universal consciousness of the whole to which we belong.

Science is objective.
Religion is blind faith.
Spirituality is complete.

Part III

Science, religion and spiritualism are three distinct domains, even though both religion and science embrace spiritualism today because of its efficacy in explaining the subject of life. Science is restricted to objects of existence, and the study of parts, using the theory of reductionism; religion believes in different gods. Spiritualism is totally opposed to the idea of a separate God. Instead, it declares that the spirit exists in a continuum in all of us. Making us aware there is a higher reality than the one we perceive through our senses, whether such higher reality is called God, spirit, soul or consciousness.

An atheist, who thrives in spiritual living, sees divinity in all that exists. Spiritualism says our sufferings are due to the separation of our energies into this and that, meaning God/Devil, truth/untruth, love/hate, etc. Unite them and accept all dualities in awareness with equal grace, and we could have a different world altogether. Today, we live by co-mingling science and religion. However, neither science nor religion have been able to provide the peace, tranquillity, love and respect for all, that we inwardly crave. Instead, we find more deception, destruction and religious divides than ever before. The answer lies in spiritualism and spiritual living; in love, grace, acceptance and awareness, as we climb the ladder of life.

If science is vital to man, the same holds true of spiritual living. If we cannot make spiritualism as inherent to us as science, we are bound to remain slaves of the mind through self-interest, desires, accumulation and attachments. The mind is primarily designed to build up the ego. Since spiritualism is experiential in nature and does not provide evidence, this declaration is regarded as a myth. In science, a declaration is considered a theory till evidence is provided to support it.

Albert Einstein commented: "A human being is part of the whole, called by us 'Universe,' a part limited in time and space. He experiences himself, his thoughts and feelings, as something separated from the rest – a kind of optical delusion of consciousness. This delusion is a kind of prison for us, restricting us to our personal desires and affection for a few persons nearest to us. Our task must be to free ourselves... by widening our circle of compassion to embrace all living creatures and the whole of nature in its beauty". Some scientists, like Erwin Schrödinger, have been awed and inspired by the *Vedanta* philosophies of the *Upanishad*s and credited these scriptures for their discoveries and pioneering work in Quantum Physics.

Quantum Mechanics (part of Quantum Physics), deals with physical phenomena at the microscopic level and says life is in motion; our minds and bodies are nothing but energy, which is constantly changing and moving. Spiritualism declares the same energy is intelligence-energy when it enters the mind and manifests as awareness. Fresh energy constantly replaces the old. As consciousness evolves, we realize life experientially. According to spiritualism, we can achieve ultimate, everlasting peace and tranquillity in Pure Consciousness or bliss. But relating such consciousness to the various gods of religion is absurd, since God is nothing but the invention of man.

Spiritualism does not believe in any single God. Originally, Hinduism was based on the divine as being omnipresent spirit or energy. But today, Hinduism has been corrupted by superstition and blind beliefs which have nullified its original ideas. Hinduism should not be considered purely as a religion or a community. It is more a philosophy and way of spiritual living.

Today, religion has taken centre stage throughout the world. Religion relies greatly on mythology which has given rise to senseless rituals and blind beliefs. These mythological stories relate to great philosophical ideas and were initially created by seers to communicate subtle truths in story form to simple people. But have now become the rigid breeding grounds of superstition and blind belief. The sublime messages of these stories have become lost and they are now just ways of creating separations. Today, we have terrorism and people mercilessly killing each other in the name of religion.

Hence, despite the progress science has brought, with religion clinging to its identifications and ego, neither has been able to bring peace and joy to mankind. This is why spiritualism has become an assertive force, even though many self-styled gurus use it as a business to gain money and fame. But when taken seriously, spiritualism does provide deep and truthful answers to the questions neglected by science and religion.

It is for us to learn, understand and experience that just as comfort, luxury or new technology are must-haves, these should be balanced with spiritual living. Otherwise, in spite of having everything, there will still be anxiety, despair and suffering. The mind alone, through its perceptual thoughts, cannot provide the peace and joy we crave.

Spiritualism declares: 'I am the Universe, because all that is, exists within me'. Whatever we need in order to attain bliss is within us; it only requires awareness to realize this. Each of us has the capacity to manifest this energy through self-awareness; retrieving it from separation into dualities by the mind. It needs to be returned to oneness. This unification cannot be achieved through self-interest, but through selfless devotion to the wholeness we are a part of. Spiritualism is not concerned with how the universe came into existence; what is important is its basis for existence. We are all energy, as spirit.

What is the purpose of this energy in human manifestation and what are the ways to achieve the ultimate goal? When the mind and body dissolve in Pure Consciousness or total awareness, this state is referred to as the Absolute or God. Attaining total awareness or pure consciousness is known as enlightenment or self-realization. For most of us, this is just a dream, a state attained by only a few and not meant for everyone. However, once one begins on this path, the journey from impure to pure is absolutely inspiring; it makes life purposeful, exhilarating and fruitful; enabling us to reach levels of fullness and wholesomeness according to our own lights.

Awareness manifests in the mind from energy – which differs greatly in humans and animals. The human brain has over a hundred billion neurons but science has yet to discover how energy manifests to become the content of our consciousness. Science believes in the theory of processes, of randomness in human evolution via various interactions. Quantum physicists have observed waves and particles of energy, and studied the sub-atomic levels of matter, which randomly and simultaneously appear here and there with no connection to space and time. On being observed, the same waves and particles become alert, as if they *know* they are being watched. Does this have any connection to the Universe or individuals being self-aware? It may seem absurd to science but in spiritualism, everything is considered to be interlinked to one source and field of unified consciousness.

Is the Universe a conscious entity? It is not, because energy only becomes aware and conscious after manifesting in the mind. Consciousness is a prerogative of the mind, through awareness, which is also a by-product of energy interacting with the mind. But the link or continuum seems to be indisputable as science too, now declares that the whole universe consists of energy which can neither be created nor destroyed and flows in one continuum.

One may say thought is what we are. Knowledge, awareness, consciousness, reasoning and intelligence, are but the interpretations of thought. Though a medium for interpretation, thought is largely dependent on external perception. Thoughts are constantly fed by data from the sensory organs and experiences; differing in every individual. The same mind and thoughts have another channel for receiving pure psychic energy – in the spontaneity of the now, through awareness.

This intelligence-energy is responsible for shaping our individuality, personality and uniqueness, depending on our degree of awareness. When the mind becomes aware of its own thoughts through inner perception, it is considered to be the Witnessing Self, the real 'I', connecting body and mind. Self-awareness is formed. Depending on each one's leanings, it either tilts towards desire and ego or towards love and compassion.

Trouble and conflicts start when thoughts are either misused or overused, relying more on external perception and less on awareness. Then the mind keeps chattering and driving us crazy. We can only free ourselves through awareness. The aware mind becomes conscious and oversees our perceptions, interpreting them through our thoughts. Consciousness becomes the master as the real Self decides and leads.

In the dialogue between science and spirituality, a rift will always remain; spiritualism being the inquiry into one's inner self, to be experienced and realized; and science relying on the outer self to quantify everything physically and mathematically, needing physical proof of what it states.

In spiritualism, consciousness is the ultimate reality, being the sum total of the subjective experiences of a person combined with the collective consciousness of the universe. Science cannot conceive of such an idea, of consciousness being connected to the cosmos; of anything being beyond the purview of the physical brain. In science, the mind is a limited entity in one brain. The thesis of every mind and brain being interconnected, interrelated and interdependent is beyond the comprehension of science.

Spiritualism explains that once the purity of consciousness is separated into dualities, there is a subject-object division in the mind, which creates the need for science and religion. One cannot survive excluding the other. In dual living, experiences are restricted to self-interest and self-consciousness, wandering from one cycle of birth and death to another, in search of purity. But when the mind becomes mindful and free of thought, experiencing without interpreting – it attains realization and enlightenment. The object (mind-body), becomes the subject in Pure consciousness, as in the case of the Buddha. It is a state of living in every single moment, where the mind and body has no relevance to the external world. It is liberation, nirvana or *moksha;* one where the subject is in complete unity and cohesion, where the object becomes meaningless. This is the experience of *Brahman* or nothingness, the unity of consciousness – when the creator emanates from creation, and becomes reality, as a complete whole.

This is not something scientists can observe through microscopes, experiments or mathematical analysis; it is purely experiential. When the observer (subject) and the observed (object), are one and the same in experiential realization, how can there be an observing mind; that too, about its own reality? The person becomes *'That'*. Being limited to objective reality, science can only interpret reality up to the level of sensation and perception.

The quantum brain or quantum consciousness is not necessarily exclusive to the mind. The seat of consciousness can arise from within or without.

Since thoughts are the accumulation of data from the past, projecting into the future, and representing the present, they become a part of our memory, which is based in nerve cells called neurons, in the subconscious mind, the storehouse of one's experiences.

Spiritualism does not debate the seat of consciousness as being the human mind or body. The mind is like an antenna or receiver of awareness from the cosmos, acting as a conduit, transmitting via thought, all that it experiences. Along with receiving such data and its reproduction into thoughts and actions, the mind functions as a processor of data received from both external and internal perceptions. This series of cumulative experiences in the mind are presumed to mature into consciousness, manifesting as 'I' and the storehouse of all we experience.

Science is mechanical.
Religion is idealistic.
Spirituality is to be alive.

Part IV

Science is a process of objective, impartial inquiry, seeking the truth behind any theory. It is open and does not believe or get carried away by beliefs; it investigates to get to the practical truth and absorbs changes over time.

In spiritualism, the truth remains the same today, as it was thousands of years ago. It believes in one reality, one truth – timeless, spaceless, changeless and limitless. This truth can be interpreted by thoughts in myriad ways.

Science is bound by facts and figures, while spiritualism is related to experience. But they cannot be utterly divorced from one another as both relate to existence – one forming the subject and the other its object. However, spiritualism can exist without science since scientific methodology is mathematical, analytical and cognitive, whereas spiritualism is meditative, experiential and seeks oneness.

Most world religions are based on concepts related to spiritualism, such as God being omnipotent, omniscient and omnipresent. This was communicated to people through simple stories by the seers of ancient times, so they could understand the complex through the simple. But as time passed, these mystical teachings became selective, authoritative and esoteric, from which religions arose.

Jesus, Buddha and Mohammed were not religious; they were realized, pure souls, spreading awareness. Then why did religions originate under the influence of their preachings? Priests and gurus made changes in what they taught, bending spiritual views in accordance with the times to gain recognition. Such preachings became the unquestioned truth for their followers and their messages became beliefs, rituals and superstitions, to fight and kill over. The real message of oneness got lost. Instead of love and compassion, jealousy and hatred of other religions developed.

Irrationality developed. People were labelled by their religious beliefs. Ego and separation ruled. No one bothered to comprehend that in the awareness of oneness, lay happiness for all. God cannot be quantified with separate names and ideas, for then he cannot be omnipresent, omnipotent and omniscient. God is purity, compassion and humility. Hence the difference: religion believes in an external God; spiritualism in the inner self; and science doubts both.

Therefore, whether God is an illusion or supreme reality is a very personal issue based on one's faith. Religion, of course, still commands a strong following. Irrespective of what we know, leaders and politicians utilize religion to arouse anger, hatred and jealousy for their own purposes – the reason we see so much violence in the name of religion.

The morality inherent in humans, however, keeps us going. Goodness, togetherness, oneness, righteousness, positivity, truth, love, sensitivity, etc., are characteristics which will always shine and remain independent of science, religion or spiritualism. In fact, this clearly shows that the goodness within us is separate from any God or religion. It is what spiritualism refers to as Self-awareness.

Today, spiritualism is treated as a serious subject. Having experienced the full spectrum of the physical world, we are gradually realizing the relevance of a spiritual path in our quest for meaning and purpose. We notice an increase in our psychological needs. We are mentally entrapped in conflicts of pleasure and pain; and anxiety, despair and suffering, due to outbursts of anger, envy, jealousy, hatred, etc. These issues demand a deeper understanding than the physical. We have to find reality and the purpose of existence in trans-materialistic comforts. There is therefore an emergence of the spirit. With the help of a realized guru or even otherwise, we can attain knowledge of the Self. From here a distinction occurs between materialistic and empirical life, through realization. We can use awareness as the pivot for our intellect and intentions, to guide us in the journey of life.

When we reach the stage of knowing, experiencing and realizing our inner perception, we also become aware of the differences between science, religion and spirituality. We gain insight and become aware of the reality in which we exist. Our physical, empirical and spiritual existence, which is based upon the difference between apparent and absolute reality give rise to questions such as: 'Who am I?'; 'Who is God?'; 'What is my purpose in living besides consuming, accumulating and wasting on mother earth?'

The three main concerns of our existence revolve around health, wealth and wisdom. After ensuring health and wealth, one should ponder the question of *who* I am. Common sense tells us that in separating ourselves through self-centeredness, from our fellow men and environment, science and religion have failed to give us the answers to the meaning of life. Instead of peace of mind, we are hurtling towards chaos and mental fatigue. Many people, who achieve stability in their lives, are then seen searching through the aisles of self-help books for guidance and answers.

Spiritualism is the opposite of the normal functioning of the mind, i.e. through sensory perceptions. It goes beyond external perceptual thoughts to the realm of awareness – making us aware and conscious through our own experiences on what we externally perceive. We begin to become aware of the mind. This inner awareness of our thoughts exists parallel to our perceptual thoughts; it witnesses the mind and forms our consciousness, resulting in focussed individuality.

The spiritual theory of reality goes further by stating that consciousness is not what is produced by the brain, but is a continuous flow of cosmic energy, manifesting in the mind as awareness. It is a continuum of all that exists. This makes it all the more relevant to deeply understand the meaning of our inner existence, where the experiential intersection of the physical, mental and spiritual takes place.

The study of Self-knowledge involves two sub-sections of our thinking process. One is based on rational or logical thinking, using scientific evidence; the other is intuitive and spontaneous awareness, using spiritual reasoning. Metaphysically, thinking in response to the data supplied by the sense organs is considered external or objective, while the data from awareness is subjective; and tells us about who and what we really are. Both these patterns of thought, the external and the internal, the rational and the spiritual, overlap while balancing each other in the manner they are experienced and realized.

Awareness is the crucial spiritual dimension upon which totality, completeness and the fullness of life is based.

In order to understand the multi-dimensional nature of reality – physical, empirical and spiritual – the wise man looks at the whole picture from a wider perspective, rather than only through the preconceived notions of science. Today, even science agrees that objective reality is an illusion. Spiritualism declares that it is only in the inner realm that one may discover the core energy, the source, consciousness, or God. But here we must reconcile science and spiritualism as both accept the existence of rational and conscious thought processes.

Even if science is at a nascent stage in the study of consciousness, the question arises, why should science and spirituality not evolve together? There is no compulsion to rely only on physical laws and banish what we feel or are conscious of. Even if collective consciousness is a far-fetched theory, why not accept the intersection between the inner and outer worlds, which falls within the realm of spiritualism, instead of pitting them against each other?

Ego is the source of our perceptions or objective reality, and consciousness becomes the source of our subjective or inner reality. They stand at opposite ends. Science finds it difficult to comprehend in the Ultimate Reality, where all meet as One; the absolute awareness which is intangible and invisible. What we need to remember is, it is only when the inner and the outer intersect, that our individuality emerges.

Spirituality is intangible; it differs in each individual in accordance to the experience, which each individual soul goes through in any existence. It manifests uniquely in each of us, depending on the degree of interaction with our body or ego-consciousness. Science is not capable of deciphering or measuring the realization of feeling in objective terms, for spiritual realization is purely subjective in each individual case.

Science has gradually come around to the idea that nature is about uncertainty and unpredictability, and operates in randomness. That was how the new science of quantum mechanics emerged. During observations, they realized that everything cannot be derived by mathematics and reductionism. When they could penetrate no further into the sub-atomic field of matter, what they discovered was that everything that exists is one, unified energy. Science is now gradually adapting to the idea that a domain deeper than what can be perceived, exists – the realm of consciousness.

The relationship between science and spiritualism is unique. They respect yet distrust each other. The respect comes from the fact that many scientists today show a keen interest in the mysticism of spiritualism and value ideas such as – the unity of existence in oneness. The main area of difference lies in their approaches to the same subject. Science relies on objective study and research, hypothesis, experimentation and inference. Spiritualism is simply concerned with the subjective aspect; claiming existence is physical, but life is purely experiential, where unity can be achieved with the infinite. The observer (subject) and the observed (object), are the same. Hence, the question of observing in such a case does not exist. Spiritualism clearly states that the infinite cannot be comprehended by the finite.

In science, the study of existence is of prime importance; spiritualism is concerned with the life that endows us with divinity. They agree that existence is interconnected, interrelated, and interdependent, forming a unified whole. But, scientific processes, even now, originate from the basic tenet of separation; between the self as observer and the Universe as object.

In spiritualism, there is no separation, seeking, or questioning; it is purely the experience of the subject, not about knowing, but realizing everything as a single unit. Scientific theories attempt to gain understanding through verifiable reality. But this reality or truth constantly changes since the thought and the thinker remain separate.

Spiritualism goes beyond, to unite this separation into one. Reality is not conceivable by the mind or science as it is subjective and experiential rather than conceptual. Anyone, applying logic, will describe reality as what our thoughts observe or can know. But the Copenhagen interpretation of quantum mechanics says that what we know is only one interpretation of reality.

The reality behind existence is Maya.
The reality behind the mind is ego.
The reality behind the Divine is consciousness.

Chapter 5
Our Reality!

Reality seems so simple yet it is highly confusing to define. Science sees reality as the actual state of objects, things that are actually experienced or seen. Hence, what we observe becomes our reality. It is based upon sensory experiences in a fixed space and time. We generally take reality to be the same for us all. Albert Einstein commented about physical reality: "Reality is merely an illusion, albeit a very persistent one."

The truth is physical reality differs for every human. We all have distinctly unique cognition of what we observe and perceive as real, through individual experiences and the sensory organs. For example, the colour green will be perceived in distinctive shades and depths, as per singular experience. Once we agree that different minds have their own distinctive experiences; can reality be what it appears to us or is there much more than meets the eye? Let us probe deeper into this question to understand what reality is all about.

Philosophers and theorists differ on this subject. Reality is multidimensional in meaning and presence. Learned men continue to debate the subject. But the scientific, merely objective definition and explanation of reality, does seem quite facile. Science is limited to physical observation through perception, but, when it comes to the subject of reality, science is silent. The meaning of reality is much wider and includes all that is tangible and intangible in our Universe, whether observable, or comprehensible, or not.

Quantum Science, on the other hand, concerns itself with the invisible world of quanta; observing everything that exists to its deepest sub-atomic depths. It defines everything as waves and particles, spontaneously sparking here and there, creating the force called energy. This also creates a multi-dimensional picture of reality in matter, far beyond what can be measured and experienced by normal sensory perceptions in space and time.

Ontology, the study of being, provides a very interesting correlation between existence as the object of reality, and consciousness and spirit as the subject of reality. It creates a clear distinction between abstract reality in consciousness and apparent reality in existence. It acknowledges a physical reality (objective), an empirical reality (experiential), and an ultimate reality (absolute, subjective or pure consciousness).

Both consciousness and physical existence manifest in the mind through thoughts, originating as awareness. The original unity gets separated into the dualities of existence; being activated as opposites. But pure consciousness retains the original oneness. In physical reality, there is cause and effect, as applied to mortal existence and changes with action-reaction. Spiritual energy, awareness, the witness, or the pure consciousness within, does not change. It remains intangible in its composition and is unaffected by cause and effect.

A clay pot has no individual existence without the presence of clay as its main observable reality. However, it can change in shape and size. In the same way, matter has no separate or real existence in the absence of its actual reality – Pure Consciousness – which is indivisible, indestructible, infinite energy.

Science remains unclear about the notion that consciousness is the fundamental reality creating our free will and individuality. Scientists continue to ponder how neural action can give rise to experience. The evidence suggests that one consciousness demodulates or even discovers the other.

Given this, we can achieve a better understanding of the second layer of reality. By penetrating into the sub-atomic structure of material objects, we can easily affirm reality is not what we see or touch. Under the facade of daily life, trillions of molecules are in motion, yet we do not recognize this reality which is happening all around and within us.

I have read that no scientist really knows what energy is exactly, except that it is a force, which is electrical, mechanical and chemical, possessing light and heat, as one field. This energy affects its magic in diverse fields – gravity, nuclear, electromagnetic – but emerges from the same source. Physicists are gradually coming to the conclusion that these fields represent a unified field, comprising one continuum.

However, there is still one other field which defies scientific definition – the intelligence comprised or embedded in and around us as unified consciousness. How this 'energy' can possess the power of intelligence or awareness of its presence, defies all scientific understanding.

This unified source of consciousness forms the fundamental basis of Ultimate Reality, in spiritualism. Rene Descartes famously pronounced: *'I think, therefore I am'*. Spiritualism declares in reverse: *I am, therefore I think*; the 'I am' refers to the

Ultimate Reality–the consciousness without which no material content can be distinguished.

To recap: we have three layers of reality, by which we discern, discriminate, and integrate in our minds, to discover answers to our questions about life. Broadly, these three layers of reality encompass our existence. The first is the observable world of material objects, which we determine through our sensory organs. The second is what we physically cannot perceive but which exists at the microscopic level in the form of frequencies and vibrations and incessant coactions of energy. The powerhouse of this flux is referred to as energy and its paramount speed is that of light. The third layer is abstract or conscious reality; the formation of experiences in the mind through awareness as Ultimate Reality.

It is only through consciousness that physical reality manifests in the mind. Mystics have said millennia ago, that the seen and unseen are the same and manifest from one source as a single field called spirit or energy. We are only now coming to accept this as the truth. They referred to it as *Brahman*; representing both the un-manifest and manifest qualities of God, pervading life.

The *Upanishads* from India claim matter is illusory and impermanent, just *maya*. There was another well-known Indian Buddhist philosopher, Vasubandhu, who lived in the 4th century CE, and claimed that all that existed was in the mind alone and what was regarded as objects or matter, was wrongly conceived.

Is matter real or not? Today, it is widely believed that matter is nothing but energy and vice versa, originating from Einstein's famous Theory of Relativity and Quantum Theory. However, science has to go further and prove that consciousness is energy. Of course, matter is real but temporary, a condensed form of organized energy in slow vibration. Energy can neither be created nor destroyed; it remains constant in any form.

The harder we try to understand consciousness, the tougher it is to comprehend. But whatever reality may be, we can agree that it is not what it seems to be, scientifically and metaphysically. It is easy to say matter is not real, but much harder to prove what it really is. Some theories claim (what spiritualism has been declaring for centuries), that reality and consciousness are one. According to the spiritualists there is only one Absolute reality that exists; all others are manifestations of the same in different forms, changing from one to another but the sum total remaining constant. The subject and the object are the same; the seen and the unseen are the same, because both have the absolute as the basic constituent.

The fact remains that whatever we consider to be matter or physical reality, is the outcome of our perceptions, which are purely mental and not material. Hence, the material world is an interplay of psychic energy, with no one to explain how perception of experience, is arrived at in the core of the mind.

Is the Self a reality? We all know that the Self is distinct from the body in which it exists. It exists in parallel to the perceptual thoughts which support existence, through experiences; subtly witnessing and guiding us physically and mentally. The Self is the unifier which brings body, mind and its surroundings together. In short, it is the experiencer (Self) – experiencing (through the mind) the experienced (physical objects).

We do notice that in reality, the Self is not just mass, a composition of matter (the body); there is also something intangible which directs both mind and body. For instance, the cells of the body keep changing, dying and being replaced, but the Self remains intact for as long as we exist. Nobody has the answer to where this Self is located. I believe the Self is the 'rememberer'; it is thus seated in the subconscious, which is the storehouse of the mind.

In the way that energy remains constant; our Self too, remains the same. But when we notice it, it keeps changing, in circles of happiness and sadness, while remaining the core which unites all into one. Self is the all-inclusive energy, which consolidates everything to become the centre of contemplation and introspection.

The Self is the light which reveals everything, awakening us from ignorance; showing us we are more than what we can physically perceive. The intuitive inner perception of ourselves, is what we really are. The constant unifier in the mind and body is the reality of the Self.

What about time? Is it real? Philosophers and scientists both agree that the present, which is now, can never be captured by the mind. It takes time for neural sensations to process experience in the mind as thoughts. By the time the now has been deciphered, time has passed and a new now has taken the place of the one that has just been processed.

Creation is the manifestation and emergence of one changeless reality, but to the perceptual mind, it represents 'change'. The mind projects change by constructing a time factor and then superimposing and conceptualizing experience according to this order. In reality, the only existence is the presence of awareness. The mind perceives this in delayed sequence, due to this time factor, only as the past or the future, not the now. Only when the mind stops relating to thoughts and observes in alertness, can it be in the present, the now. The connection between the past, present and future, in totality, is the required spiritual energy for completion, in oneness.

So how do we determine which time is real – the past, present or future? The time we are accustomed to is manmade, objectively perceived in space for a specified, measurable duration. But it is not the fundamental and subjective time which is its real essence, as revealed by the changeless presence of the now.

The spiritual is the presence of any moment which is real. When the now happens in the presence of something, it is all that exists. Our perceptions and thoughts alone can at most, connect us to the past. It is only through the *experience* of the moment that we can be in the now.

Thoughts or knowledge can only reveal what was already known in the past or can think about the future based on past knowledge, which has nothing to do with the now. Awareness, which spontaneously arises in the present moment, exhibits intuitiveness and creativity, which gets converted into thoughts. So we are ultimately left with only the now, which is present from one moment to the next, as the core reality; termed mindfulness, in spiritualism.

Reality is connected to both our apparent and inner perceptions of what we see and experience. The external perception of reality has been negated by science; which has proven that reality is not what it seems. However, science remains limited to simple, objective reality, because it can measure, experiment and infer only what can be perceived. It shies away from matters relating to subjective reality.

Spiritualism, on the other hand, defines reality as three aspects: 1. Illusory 2. Empirical or experiential and 3. Absolute. In spiritualism, the moment is not divided into parts; it is a complete whole and changeless. Illusory reality and experiential reality are both prone to change due to cause and effect.

In spirituality, reality is static at its integral level. Money, time, a clay pot, waves in the ocean, all these are not basic and hence prone to change. Reality is that which is permanent and cannot change. If it did, it would be deemed apparent reality. Love, truth, the now, pure consciousness, etc. are absolute examples of changeless reality. They reveal their presence but do not change in space or time.

However, if separated from their absoluteness, into dualities, they become apparent. For example, the truth becomes a lie and vice versa. Quantum Science declares energy to be the Ultimate Reality; that all that exists is nothing but energy, which can neither be created nor destroyed. Spiritualism calls this *Brahman* – where energy remains static in its own identity and presence. On separating from its core equilibrium, it becomes dynamic and accretes into parts.

Potential energy turns into kinetic energy; intrinsically remaining the same, but changing through motion and interactions with its surroundings, like thermal to electrical energy. Similarly, consciousness is potentially changeless but in interacting with the mind, creates changes (as from child-consciousness to ego-consciousness), and the mind becomes the dynamic power forming our personality. Both mind and matter are apparent realities, existing within a third potential energy called Pure Consciousness, which separates into dualities to direct our existence and the experience of happiness and sorrow.

Many scientists may disagree with the fundamental or subjective reality of the Absolute, but they agree that sensory organs perceive only material objects that exist in impermanent extrinsic forms and not in their intrinsic character. Every single thing that exists on this earth has an apparent or interim form within the Absolute.

Therefore, I repeat: reality has three different aspects – one is illusory, being individual; the second is empirical, when experiences take place; and the third is the Absolute. Through superimposition, this indivisible absolute seems apparently divisible. Vedanta declares this Pure Consciousness, the non-perceivable Absolute, to be the Ultimate Reality.

Life cannot be restricted to birth and death.
It existed before birth and will exist after death.

Chapter 6
What exactly is Life?
Part I

What is life? It sounds like a strange question. Even scientists have a tough time describing life. Biology describes existence as a process of vigorous change at the cellular level of our DNA, involving millions of cells every day. But the psychic experiences and changes the mind undergoes, confuses all branches of science. Despite the remarkable progress of science and technology, the mysteries behind life continue to baffle mankind. We struggle to understand the basic constituents of life – its source, its continuity and what happens after death.

Science has another limitation. Its methodology is based mainly on the physicality and matter of objects. It functions on the theory of reductionism, from which it derives material inferences and objective analyses. Take for example the concept of the afterlife. It is something that has puzzled both scientists and the devout, for aeons. What science requires is evidence. Since it has yet to decipher even how our neural network derives experience, the forever-nebulous questions of life, death and the afterlife seem destined to remain mysteries to science.

But mystics, over the centuries, have provided incisive and lucid answers to the complexities which surround our existence. Ancient Eastern spiritualism states that life is nothing but a series of experiences which the mind goes through after attaining immediate awareness; forming the content of what we call consciousness. Existence is sustained as long as the mind can manifest energy into awareness – to be conscious and to experience – and till the body breathes. When both stop, death occurs.

The Ultimate Reality is nothing but the divine energy, spirit and awareness, called *Brahman*. It pervades, permeates and penetrates all that exists in the universe. *Brahman* simply flows through a series of experiences in awareness, forming consciousness, from which we form our observable reality through perception.

But the reality in our mind is only apparent reality or illusion, created by what the mind perceives. Seeing, hearing, smelling, tasting and touching, are just interpretations by the mind. Even the Universe can only be described as *shunya* or nothingness, unless the mind gives it an image and name, interpreting what we call energy or reality in the same way as the mind interprets that the earth is not flat but round and that the sun does not move, other bodies move around it. This ancient doctrine further claims that *Brahman* is spaceless, timeless, limitless and changeless – the ultimate in absolute, non-dual, radiant energy.

All that we perceive and conceive are but apparent manifestations of our own mind. A division is thus created between existence and life. In the former, we have the body and mind existing in the apparent reality of birth and death and biological existence. In the latter, we have the absolute as the luminous eternal energy, flowing in transcendence beyond the subject-object relation, in continuation from one cycle of birth and death to another, witnessing in the form of consciousness. Hence, consciousness comes from nothing, which in fact is everything. Scientists call it dark energy. There is no such thing as nothingness because, in fact, it is 'allness' that actually exists throughout.

Consciousness, within the framework of the body and mind, changes according to its purity. When it tilts towards the dualities of existence, it is referred to as ego; if not, it is pure consciousness. In both cases, consciousness merges with life to become eternal, in unified consciousness. In this manner, the body and mind decompose but the soul, spirit or consciousness transmigrates to within that 'allness', into another existence, in order to revive its journey, until it finally reaches its destination, complete, having travelled from ego to purity, from separation to unification, back into One.

Quantum physics and the conservation of energy are both in consonance with the spiritual doctrine that all that exists is energy, which can neither be created nor destroyed; that mass and energy remains equal and constant. It can change form; potential to kinetic, from mass to liquid or gas, but the total energy remains constant and independent of any changes. Therefore, within this parameter of the conservation of energy, as long as the body breathes and the mind experiences external and internal perceptions, existence is said to be complete and alive, with the total energy remaining constant, regardless of the changes occurring within. When the mind stops experiencing and the body stops breathing, we are termed 'dead', transforming into another form of energy.

The functioning of the mind commences with the conversion of raw energy into awareness, forming the content of our consciousness; drawing from a series of experiences. In this way the mind becomes aware and conscious of what it thinks, forms intentions using past awareness embedded in memory, and combines with the reasoning of the intellect, to experience life.

Thus the mind creates consciousness through awareness of all that it perceives and experiences of existence – space, time, love, truth, the Universe, etc. – forming empirical reality. Everything that exists is thus the manifestation of the mind and neural vision, creating observable or perceptual reality.

Our perceptions and experiences conceive of the notions of birth, death and everything else that exists. These are nothing but the neural inventions or figments of imagination of our consciousness, ignited when the mind converts energy into awareness. The body and brain decompose and become another form of energy, but the conscious and aware energy of the mind keeps floating and attracting other consciousness — intermingling, interconnected, interdependent and interrelated to a unified source; transmigrating from one cycle of birth and death to another.

Therefore, life is an adventurous journey in which the waves and particles of energy, at the sub-atomic level, simultaneously change. They are not bound to time or space but are alert, forming experiences through the mind, which we refer to as consciousness. Life transcends our inner and outer perceptions of existence. It is a universe of waves and particles which move in bizarre fashion, but in the unity of oneness. Such quantum consciousness is referred to as the cosmic dance of Shiva (*Natraja*). In Eastern spiritualism, this is the ecstatic dance of absolute non-dual energy.

If the theory of energy in Quantum Mechanics is of any significance, we cannot rule out perpetuity or the afterlife of individual consciousness. If the body and mind decompose and become energy in a different form, intelligence-energy, comprising consciousness, cannot simply wither away into oblivion. It is bound to flow with its own data of intelligence-energy in quantum consciousness.

When it comes to intangible subjects like God, consciousness, the soul or even the physical experience of life, it is left to philosophers and mystics to elaborate upon them. The basis of science is physics and mathematics, which deal primarily with the physicality of matter; they do not offer concrete answers on the nature of experience.

Because of this, we have achieved significant understanding of the objective aspects of existence. But science has failed to understand anything as a whole or in totality, leaving space for new interpretations. That is why truth, reality and every inference keep changing as scientific understanding evolves. Science is basically the study of gross, physical structures and their functioning within a specified space and time in interactions with the objective world. But life itself is based on the source and flow of mind, matter and energy.

Nobel Laureate and renowned scientist, Erwin Schrödinger, attempted to explain the meaning of life in his lectures delivered under the auspices of the Dublin Institute for Advanced Studies, in February 1943. He realized scientific knowledge was based upon perception and resulted in mathematical, analytical and cognitive outcomes limited to physicality.

However, when human intelligence functioned via the experiences of physical/non-physical properties, it went beyond thought and perception in matter, to aware-conscious experience. It is like another witness appearing within the same mind and realizing that the 'I am' is separate/different from its own perceptive mind. Spiritualism refers to this as consciousness or the real Self, emerging from awareness, in an individual's mind.

Schrodinger had to substantiate his study with the mystical philosophies of the East. He gives credit to the *Upanishads* in his book, *What is Life?*, explaining that life differs from the physical aspect and is innate experience. Aldous Huxley mentioned his point of view in his, *The Perennial Philosophy,* a study on religions.

Apart from our mechanical and physiological existence, when we introspect or contemplate, we discover a subtle witnessing force within. It runs parallel to our perceptive thoughts but is a separate composition of thoughts originating from our experiences, telling us what we see, hear or touch is not decided by the perception of the sense organs but the experiential 'I am,' which makes us what we really are.

These innate experiences do not follow any fixed pattern and go beyond the laws of objectivity and the physicality of science. Consciousness is based on such experiences in individuals, always in the singular. Thus, individuals have their unique self-awareness, and this gradually forms their inner-identity, personality and individuality.

Awareness observes through the perceptive mind, internally and externally, but all changes are made as manifestations of the mind, making us aware and conscious of what we perceive. Awareness goes beyond subject-object affinity, without reference of opposites.

On the other hand, mind and existence can function only in plurality or dualities — good/bad, positive/

negative, God/Devil, etc. — forming desires, attachments and ego in pure self-interest while discerning, discriminating and choosing.

Consciousness, through awareness and experiences, awakens us to the reality that we are not just the body, mind or a bundle of desires. We are one, indivisible energy in which oneness has been separated into two, creating an existence of dualities, positive and negative. It reminds us that the purpose of life is to accept both with grace and awareness and in the totality of oneness.

Therefore, one's experiences become a part of memory, creating a link between the individual and cosmic energy in the subconscious mind. It defines the individual. Whether in dreaming, sleeping or waking states, this self-subconscious determines one's real identity. But, while an individual may physically die, his self-identity remains in perpetuity, as living memory. While the soul joins the great, unified consciousness, the individual continues to be remembered for his uniqueness.

Spiritualism declares that Pure Consciousness is God – the witnessing force of life, which counters thoughts of illusion in the mind. It acts as the chisel, which sculpts the physical mind and body while bringing the personality within to wisdom. Spiritually, consciousness prevails only in self-awareness that enables us to conquer any object of existence. For example, if we find a wallet has fallen from the coat of a person ahead, we pick up the wallet and immediately two simultaneous thoughts emerge: one says to return the wallet (consciousness), while the other argues against it (perceptive mind). The first is referred to as the real Self or the life within existence; the latter is the false self – the sensuous perceptions of the mind.

What we need to remember here is that when we see with our eyes, light rays enter as impulses and are interpreted by the cognitive mind to assist us in seeing objects. However, what we see (physically) and what we wish to see (through mind) may not be the same.

Immediate and spontaneous awareness of the now, using creativity and past awareness make us conscious of what the mind has perceived. Both are influenced by our personal power and distinct individuality, to create common sense, and through the intellect and its power of reasoning, determine the final outcome of any impulse, sensation, impression or observation.

Thus, the brain and body, as objects, cannot entirely make the subjective 'I' see the perspective it wishes to see through external perception – unless 'I', through its own consciousness or individuality, does so. We are normally dependent on the sense organs with respect to external perceptions, allowing the outer constructs of the mind to rule and influence us, in the form of ego.

This becomes the primary cause of our anxieties and suffering. Science cannot relate to this or define the experiential part of subjective experience, which the mind goes through. We need to remember the presence of the conscious mind – our real, Witnessing Self – behind all that the mind does.

To summarize: consciousness is always experienced in self-awareness. In this way, it retains the personal identity of the individual, like beads strung upon a necklace, in one complete whole of unified consciousness. Thinking, through outer perception, merely separates absolute energy into plurality or duality. To rectify this, we have awareness, through which, we can bring dualities closer to their oneness. Else we continue to exist with illusion and suffering.

Scientific knowledge is dependent on physical properties derived by observation through the sense perceptions. To claim the evidential presence of consciousness as a unit of energy is beyond its capacity as it reveals no physicality or objective characteristics. As in the physical experience of seeing colour, the personal perception of shade and depth cannot be calculated or measured by science.

The paradox of life – we live with inner ugliness in the disguise of external beauty.

Part II

As discussed in Part I, the meaning of life is not what it seems. Science does not have a definition and includes existence and life under one heading. We have discussed the aims of spiritualism, connecting consciousness to life, to finally evolve and join the unified consciousness in eternity. Science is concerned with biological or objective existence, where we need to be physically present in order to exist. Metaphysically, life is the presence of our being, which is not perishable, as is the body and mind, but is immortal though awareness. It does not change its reality with age and time.

The perceiver remains separate as long as he exists as body and mind. He becomes the perceived when these dissolve in total awareness or Pure Consciousness. Life exists empirically, as the witnessing Self; enabling us to get back to the totality of completeness and continue to flow along with the unified consciousness, where birth and death are but a part of the journey.

When such a complex topic is touched upon, it is best to discuss it from all points of view – philosophical, spiritual and scientific. Here, we delve further into the mystery behind life as explained by mystics, taking a scientific approach when required. This is because of the limitations of science with regards to the subject of life; spiritualism or even ontology provides deeper answers.

Let us start at the source of intelligence-energy or the light of life. Instead of approaching the subject with the mind, let us for moments consider the manner in which our eyes perceive light. The quantum of light is everything, from which everything originates in the mind. Everything we see and observe starts with light. It is the source of awareness, the information the mind receives, and also the first communion, starting from the eyes and beaming energy to activate innumerable actions in other parts of the body and mind. Many scientists agree that matter is nothing but energy or condensed light in slow vibration.

Light precedes everything. In fact, it is the source of life. The energy of light finally settles, as consciousness, having as its seat the memory centres in our subconscious. The *Vedas* consider this self-luminous consciousness the Light of Lights and the source of all knowledge.

To elaborate on the subject of light I refer to one of the oldest divine hymns, the *Gayatri Mantra,* which is based on a Sanskrit verse from the *Rigveda* (3.62.10): *Let us adore the supremacy of that divine sun, the god-head which illuminates all, who recreates all, from whom all proceed, to whom all must return, whom we invoke to direct our understandings aright in our progress toward his holy seat.* [Translated by Sir William Jones, 1807.] Hindus have chanted this mantra for 5000 years, as a prayer to the Supreme Self to manifest pure wisdom in our lives through light.

Just as truth and happiness can be expressed but not defined, likewise, life is an experience, we cannot capture in words and thoughts. Spiritualism, unlike science, knows life is limitless, spaceless, timeless and changeless. It is the light that reveals all objects. Life is not an object we can dissect. It is the reality of awareness. It is consciousness and inner perception.

Light is the source of luminosity in life. Life and light are inter-linked – both reveal the object and subject of every form of knowledge. It does not require psychophysical or physiological intervention to understand the source of life as being the reality behind the subject-object relationship.

Life is intelligence energy derived from a series of experiences in existence. We evolve through that Consciousness into individuals, referred to in spiritualism as the real or witnessing Self. From creating biological life to primitive intelligence, light is responsible for everything that has evolved.

In this manner, something came from nothing – the Big Bang theory.

Returning to our subjective topic of life, we know that the sense organs, while they provide external perceptions to the mind, are restricted to respective objects. This is where a distinction can be drawn between existence and life. Existence is connected with the physical self, objectively, relying on sense perceptions, whereas life is solely the subject of being.

Thoughts are identified with the physical aspects of growth and decay of the body and mind, living an illusory life in relativity or duality. Here, truth, reality and God are related to their opposites. However, in existence, one is only aware of the outer self and personality is formed based entirely on self-interest or ego.

The *Upanishads* declare that the sense organs are limited to the physical, objective form. They function as intermediaries to determine inferences and exist only in duality. But we are all one, not two. Besides external perceptions, sensations or experiences, we also have a higher witnessing Self, observing and guiding all that we know, act, remember, experience and realize, without objective mediation from any external field. Here, the sense organs play no role. Memory emerges, making us aware and conscious of who we are, what we know, and how we should act. This internal knower is the sum total of our external (objective) and inner (subjective) awareness and consciousness. Each separate nuance of defined consciousness, tied together in continuity, like a necklace, signifies the whole of unified consciousness.

Therefore, life is the sum total of both external and internal experiences of the mind, based within the subconscious, on a series of experiences which forms our individual self-awareness, individuality and personality.

The body is the temple and mind the devotee. The soul or life is God, residing within and telling us who we really are. Thoughts play a role only as a medium to interpret what consciousness and intellect determine.

By now you will have realized why seemingly simple things in life are so complex. I have combined science and spiritualism to elaborate on what life is. We will now discuss the interesting topic of how to exist in life.

One may acquire money, fame and wealth, but there will always be emptiness within us, insecurity, despite having everything. We will keep wanting more and more to feed our insecurities. However, the more we have, the more insecure we become – because in all this materialism, the mind may be present, but our real presence is missing. This presence, our being, which makes us alive, is what spiritualism is all about.

Life demands too much from us. If God is complete and we are a part of Him, then He too, is incomplete without us. Until we merge our energy and dissolve the ego through selflessness, compassion and non-attachment, the God within us remains unrealized. Meaning, 'thou art that, but cannot be That'. This is asking for too much; it is rare and not achievable by the average person. For this reason, we have people like Buddha and Christ appearing once in a thousand years or so.

We exist through the separation of life energy from its absoluteness, into dualities, dichotomies and opposites. But each opposite cannot exist without the other, as they are part of the same thing. It is awareness and conscious reality that brings forth the idea of material existence. We are all so engrossed in worldly life that we forget the God within; the witnessing Self, to whom we shut our mind, ears and eyes, experiencing only the illusions of materialism.

Is this a cosmic joke? Are the seers, sages, gurus and religious preachers correct in formulating a long list of do's and don'ts, which inspire and invigorate high ideals in the mind, but are so difficult to experience and practice? The fact remains that when we penetrate deep into the Self, there is an emptiness which is paradoxically full.

Spirituality cannot be taught, passed on, preached or even read about; we need to experience and realize it through living. While we need to first learn and understand what Self-knowledge is, beyond that, it is all-experiential. Knowledge is never complete unless experienced. That is where the real 'I', our consciousness and individuality come in.

Because knowledge gained from someone else's experience would be different to what I go through myself, these made me seriously ponder the subject of spiritualism on my own, without seeking advice from anyone else. This was my first lesson: Self-knowledge is no use if not personally experienced.

Fancy books and lectures are like watching a good movie on a fine evening and forgetting it the next day or glorified in conversations for a few days: Oh, what a great movie! Knowledge is only worthy when awareness dawns and percolates into your consciousness in actual practice in experiencing and knowing. It is only spiritualism, which insists that life is experiential-living, and Self-knowledge is a tool to awaken us from worldly ignorance.

Secondly, what I learnt through spiritualism is, from the experiences and knowledge that we have gained with respect to the inner sense, evolves that spiritual awareness which creates our consciousness. This needs to be taken seriously, otherwise the internal and the external worldly experiences will leave us standing on the edge of an abyss, neither able to jump across nor go any further in our presence in life. We need to know our inner self, in honesty, and not self-judge any situation.

Spirituality teaches us the need to introspect, contemplate and meditate regularly, to get to know the real Self within. Consciousness keeps changing in the mind with every single experience, making us realize and evolve through wisdom. We need to circumvent the mind, quieten our thoughts from wandering into past and future through watchfulness, observance, alertness and awareness, from one moment to the next in order to capture the present moment, which thought is incapable of doing.

The third point of spiritualism is the most difficult – what path to follow if we wish to attain comfort, peace and tranquillity. On one hand, we have the material world with all its demands, desires and expectations, and on the other, we have experiential and transcendental knowledge telling us everything is an illusion. We can balance our life with unconditional love and acceptance of everything.

By practicing the points mentioned above; the sense of 'Self' begins to transform from content to context, in the fourth dimension – towards the infinite and transcendental state of *turiya*. Spiritualism is the only medium which covers the totality of life through yoga, meditation and *Ayurveda* – how to align the body, mind and soul; and methods to live spiritually. It approaches life physically, psychologically, psychosomatically, materialistically and philosophically.

I learnt that besides financial, social, physical and mental needs, there was one other aspect to be looked into. The subtle, witnessing Self, hiding within us has all the answers. It is the real Self or consciousness. What we need to learn is how to converse and respond to that consciousness. Successful people have excelled in their field of worldly expertise; but are they really successful in every aspect of life?

Are they aligned physically, financially, socially and mentally? Are they genuinely content and at peace with themselves? This is what our purpose in life should be – wholesome success, complete and aware.

Only spiritualism is capable of providing such a life. It is probably for this reason that the *Vedas* provided four main requisites for life, which are as relevant today as when the Vedas were written. The first three are for worldly life: righteousness, economic well-being, and sensuous desires. The fourth cannot be easily defined or described: liberation or *moksha*. It is purely spiritual and refers to experiential living through the soul in order to find liberation from the other three. It is only meant for those who are able to dissolve their body and mind through awareness into their soul, in order to experience and realize pure consciousness. Buddha realized enlightenment through experiential living. *Moksha,* like love, truth, and God, is a direct experience in its realization.

Life is uncertain. Death is certain.

Chapter 7
Death

For years I have been writing and researching about life and consciousness; elaborating on the significance of self-knowledge, self-awareness and self-realization. Then it struck me that to learn the meaning of life, we should also know about death. I also realized that these three books on the spiritual aspects of life would be incomplete without dealing with the subject of death for if there is anything certain in this existence, it is death.

If existence dictates we are born only to decay and decompose one day, then why bother to know about Supreme Reality, consciousness, God, our purpose in life, etc.? What is the point to all this if we are going to die anyway? What difference does it make, despite all our efforts to know and practice spiritualism? There is no telling how much suffering we may have to endure before going back whence we came.

It is said that all life on earth will eventually be wiped out, as the sun becomes a red giant, engulfing everything. Even the Universe will be unable to sustain life, fusing all matter and energy into a final Big Crunch. Life will disappear and only potential or kinetic energy, in the form of solids, liquids and gases, will remain. If life is destined to be blotted out, does death in fact make life meaningless? If a ventilator is what we finally end up with, why strive to know that all that exists is *Brahman* (energy), liberation (*nirvana*), and pure consciousness?

First, we need to know that existence does not need to be immortal or everlasting to be meaningful. Secondly, our real journey is not about longevity but to know, experience and realize how and where the supreme mind takes us on a roller-coaster ride of happiness/sadness, God/Devil, truth/untruth, etc. making us ponder, enjoy, outgrow and transform in all sorts of ways, depending on our personal capacity.

All of us fear death to some extent. Despite knowing we are all mortal; we behave as though we are never going to die. When death comes, we are caught unawares. We were not born to necessarily fulfil any great purpose; neither is our existence a part of a greater meaning. Probably, this is why most people consume and accumulate selfishly, all that comes their way. The reverse takes place when we are in trouble, depressed, anxious or weak. Then in fear, we tend to blindly follow traditions, dogma, caste, creed, God, spiritualism and other beliefs, to sustain us.

In this rat race, our wants are never going to cease; with every pleasure, there is pain lurking behind, taking us on a roller-coaster ride, until death. Death is the ultimate certainty that makes everything we cling to vanish. In fact, death is our constant shadow. What we build today is gone tomorrow, because death destroys in order to bring in the new. The present dies, becomes the past, to bring in the future. Millions of cells keep dying, to be replaced by new ones. We are so busy accumulating things and fulfilling our desires, attachments and sentiments, we forget death is a constant presence.

Nobody will ever know for certain whether we are here for a higher purpose. But whether our life has been meaningful to us before we die is purely dependent on our own judgement and the values we attribute to life, rather than those borrowed from or acquired by listening to others. Our own personality is the result of what we believe in as individuals and not what we blindly follow.

From childhood onwards we are dictated to and conditioned by our parents, teachers, friends, spouse, society, elders, gurus, preachers and so on, about what, how and when, anything to everything. This results in a 'borrowed' personality, which only seems to want what we do not have or become someone else. We spend our energies thinking, talking and following others, ignoring our own self. We live under the influence of others and prove to our shallow ego that we are always right, living and experiencing with our cumulating beliefs.

We are what we believe, which turns into belief creating that intention to indulge and experience. Therefore we are programmed with a whole lot of beliefs out of which it is said that only 5% comes out to what we want and the remaining comes from what has been conditioned or downloaded by others especially during our 0-5 years when we were not aware, and all that was told by parents, teachers, preachers and friends were taken as gospel truth.

The power of belief, if it says you can do something, the mind gets programmed accordingly and functions in that manner. Say your positive belief will start to draw extra energy utilizing reserve cells to repair and replace, as long as the focus and intention remains intact on that subject.

In our mind there is a clear segregation between the conscious and the sub-conscious. The conscious part is hardly used by 5%, which has all your wants, wishes, desires attachments aspirations etc. The sub-conscious, the center for storage of data as memory is the driving machine from where all the collective beliefs pour out, consuming 95% of your mind.

Therefore, your whole personality revolves around on the reflexes of your sub-conscious, either spontaneous or conditioned, whether it is functioning out of blind beliefs by others or through immediate awareness with your own reasoning in intuitive common sense.

This is where the deepest secret behind body, mind and soul lies and is that concrete answer pertaining to the art of rightful living. Why is it that spiritualism insists on awareness as the primary source of intelligence energy? If 95% is conditioned memory, going back generations, and if our own creative mind, which is responsible for making our uniqueness, is left to only 5%, then only spiritual awareness is capable of functioning in the mind as a saving grace, to enhance that conscious part or 5%, in the now, to expand our personality and thereby our consciousness, towards righteousness.

The role of awareness is the only answer to bring forth the real 'you' and 'I' together, alienating you from the past orientation or desiring with respect to future in order to awaken you into the now, in the presence of your conscious mind and not on beliefs with experiences of others. I repeat, in order for the awareness to percolate into your conscious mind to form your consciousness, it has to be in the presence of the now, because the conditioned mind is already burdened and embalmed with that of the past.

Internally, we want everything for 'me and mine'; outwardly, we project a concerned and god-fearing attitude. That hypocrisy is applicable to most of us. It clearly shows we need to create our own meaning for life, if we wish to exist in a worthy and wholesome manner. There is much more to life than our never-ending desires, the aim being to transcend but not to repent, regret or resent what we think, feel and experience during life.

Without going into their philosophical, religious, idealistic or theological connotations, let us discuss in the most practical way, the meaning of life and death. First and foremost, the meaning and purpose of life is expressed through health, wealth and the wisdom to discover the most creative, individual, practical and positive ways to fulfil our lives and feel wholesome and complete.

To do so we must exist experientially, rather than following the herd and blindly saying, 'yes' or 'no'. When one achieves success in family, society and morality, one finds a deeper meaning to life, in completeness. The zest of life is in being able to accept and smile at ourselves, and courageously face unfavourable circumstances instead of complaining about them. If we appreciate and are content with what we have; if we love and respect others; there will be much greater peace in accepting death when it comes. Existence teaches us how to thrive in life; wisdom teaches us how to live and then accept death, crushing ego to attain fullness in life.

My own experience of the spiritual life began after I had gained the necessities of existence, with the question: 'Now what?' There was something still lacking, quite apart from my wants, needs and greed. I began the journey to gain neutral vision, to know and understand the meaning of self-actualization.

For me, spiritualism was the answer to all my questions about life and death. The precondition is, to not get carried away by gurus, or preachers. By believing or following them blindly we keep going in circles, never reaching anywhere; only enhancing the ego. Being on our own, we may not get all the answers, but we are bound to find many solutions through our own experiences to improve and transcend life, in a manner we can be proud of, and face whatever life or death has in store for us.

I was once asked by a famous blogger writer to comment on his blog post titled, 'Do We Really Need God?' The answer I provided, I strongly feel, is also the answer to every question related to life or death: 'Awareness is that ultimate luminous energy which connects us to God, within and without. God is an experience; an intensely inner experience. The more we have of such experience, the higher will be the completeness within us in terms of both life and death. It is entirely up to us and our deeds, how much we need Him.'

Consciousness is just a bundle of desires, unless awareness enters to guide us in the direction of meditation and living from one moment to the next in mindfulness, connected to our inner reality, rather than exhibiting outwardly what we are not. After all, if what we are searching for is within us and awareness is the primary answer, then why seek so many things? The main thing is to be honest to ourselves. In this way we grow as individuals who are unafraid of living or dying.

As we gain in strength, we realize that being true to ourselves cannot be taught; it can only be experienced through awareness. If we wish to stop smoking, suppression will not work unless we become aware, every time we light a cigarette, of the damage it is causing. Only then can we wean ourselves away from the habit.

For existence to be meaningful, it is not necessary for it to last forever. Duration has no connection to the manner in which we spend our days. In fact, life is so precious to us, that even on our deathbed we cling to it. The secret of letting go lies in knowing, understanding and then transcending both life and death.

We are familiar with the teachings that the real Self does not die; that there is life after death; that consciousness transmigrates to be reborn in another body as per our *karma*. These things are certainly taught in our ancient doctrines. Here, however, our concern is with our present, experiential existence and its decomposition. This is not to disregard spiritual literature but to discuss methods to achieve fullness in life in order to be able to accept death when it comes.

Philosophy is meaningless unless we are true to and aware of our own selves. Thereby, the law of righteousness prevails and reduces the evil within us. This humanistic issue is the essence of life, and the most difficult to achieve. In life, we keep making excuses and do not remain true to our consciousness, proving that both the Devil and God exist in our minds. It is only through awareness that we can be true to the self, and thus gain a realistic picture of life and death. Awareness teaches us that existential acceptance through righteousness is the answer rather than brooding, grumbling or striving for control. What we require is an acceptance with gratitude in order to outgrow from what we disapprove and transform with a positive attitude, rather than control or suppression to soothe your ego.

There are many reasons for fearing death. The existential fear of death may be the hardest to conquer, as compared to the fear of pain one may face while passing away. We may also fear separation from our near and dear ones or the feeling of losing everything we have accumulated in life. Fear can also stem from anxiety about who will take care of us when we are about to depart this life.

We need awareness to tackle all these fears, which spring from deep within the cognitive mind and accept that all living creatures must die. It may even help us to sort out issues which we may otherwise overlook – like giving back something to the environment or planning ahead so that those close to us are not burdened by our passing.

Self-actualization is awareness and acceptance of the realities of life and death, without resentment or regret – acceptance with grace and respect. I understand the ontological assertions about an afterlife and the immortality of consciousness where our *karmas* decide whether we rise or fall. In these theories, fear of death is covered up with the sheath of faith and belief, not realizing that heaven or hell lies within us in life itself. It is for the individual to be righteous and decide his degree of belief in every issue related to life and death; and whether he needs to derive courage through blind beliefs or by awareness. As long as we have an open mind, an appreciative heart, and an aware consciousness, both life and death can be faced with equanimity.

Spirituality plays a big role in changing our attitude towards death; subtly leading us towards awareness and oneness. As we gain such knowledge; practice, experience, and realize its methods of guidance, we become individuals who live fully and do not fear death.

The soul neither exists nor dies.
The soul is neither your body nor mind.
The soul can neither be created nor destroyed.
The soul remains constant.
Forever dancing in awareness.

Chapter 8
What Is Consciousness?
Part I

For thousands of years, philosophers, spiritualists, scientists and theorists have grappled with the phenomena of consciousness but the mystery persists. Neuroscientists still wonder how billions of tiny neural cells can produce subjective experience, interconnecting the physical and psychic realms of the mind.

Where does consciousness originate? Does it dissolve after death into nothingness or does it transmigrate into another being? Even if it transmigrates, how does it multiply to keep up with the rampant increase in population? These questions still have no concrete answers.

What is consciousness? We are all conscious – physically, psychologically and spiritually. Consciousness is the state of being aware. Many people equate consciousness with self-awareness, when in fact it is being aware of the inner being in relation to its outer surroundings. Philosophers relate consciousness to the relationship of awareness between the mind and the external world. Medicine relates consciousness to patient responsiveness. Spirituality relates consciousness to God, the inner truth, and the reality of who we are. Thus there is a clear distinction between ordinary and spiritual consciousness.

There are various states of consciousness within philosophical, scientific and spiritual paradigms: *Simple Consciousness,* or awareness of the body, as possessed by animals; *Consciousness,* or awareness of being aware, as possessed only by humans; *Altered State Of Consciousness,* when brain activity is induced by drugs, hypnosis or transcendental meditation; *Spiritual Consciousness,* when the mind is in a meditative state of awareness in the present moment, without allowing thoughts to disturb this serenity by going into the past or the future.

Spiritualism declares that consciousness is the content of what we are; science claims these are subjective experiences, unique in each of us, giving rise to internal and external factors. Spiritualism claims we are not the body but pure intelligent-energy, in the form of total awareness or pure consciousness. Awareness, on manifesting within the mind, makes the mind conscious and merges with intellect, through reason. Consciousness is what we are. These are exclusive subjective experiences unique to us, giving rise to external and internal factors. It is only when we are conscious that material reality and external perceptions emerge.

How do these experiences arise from a physical brain? Science has yet to determine the relationship and functioning between the tangible and intangible realms in which we exist, between the brain, mind and body. Science is open to theories, as long as they can be proven. Extensive research is ongoing in psychology and neuroscience to understand consciousness at the biological and psychological levels. Science, restricted to what it can see and observe, is hard pressed to understand how a brain, composed of billions of neurons, can create a network of infinite neural interconnections. How does it produce subjective experiences, which can witness physical and mental experiences in parallel?

When a sperm fertilizes an egg, existence begins, condensing more and more energy to change and mutate in shape and size. As one grows, intelligent-energy emerges entering the mind, manifesting as awareness, and then merging with reasoning to make us conscious. Life is the bridge between breathing and consciousness, with the outer, cosmic spirit connecting the two.

Before the emergence of consciousness, there is no duality, time or space. There is no separation of energy into this or that, no distinction or identification. Consciousness is thus the basic fact of life in experiencing the dual and realizing the non-dual. Absolute energy becomes two-fold in the presence of the mind, designed to discern, discriminate and choose for its own self-interest, whatever the mind perceives. Existence continues with duality at its centre and remains that way till the body and mind decompose.

As long as the mind is not fully aware, ideas, thoughts and images keep churning in the mind. The body and mind are like waves in the ocean – they come and go, changing constantly, to finally dissipate, having no permanent reality. In such existence, the realm of consciousness is limited to space and time.

Spiritualism claims that awareness is the presence of who we really are. It is through awareness that consciousness emerges to form the basis of what we are. This consciousness – a part of unified consciousness and complete whole – may change in the mind, but it also remains changeless as the Witnessing Self; transmigrating, the moment breath ceases, entering into another.

The mind receives data and processes the same with inner and outer perceptions. Awareness is the experiencer which screens this process and distinguishes itself from the inner self. Between the reception of any input by the mind and its reproduction after processing, there is a loss of time, between input and output. This loss stops the mind from capturing the present moment; hence the interpreter of thoughts reflects only the past, projecting into the future, and forms subtle layers of duality in ego-consciousness upon the core being of the pure Witnessing Self.

Spiritual living peels off the strata of such layers formed by the ego-mind and it reduces the process of separating energy into two. Thoughts relate to whatever has already happened, creating content and memories about the body, senses, emotions, family, friends, house and so on. This sort of identification is related to ownership by the mind, forming layers of self-consciousness based on ego. Ego, in its focus on 'me, mine and myself', starts believing itself to be separate, with its own existence, thereby inviting conflicts and ailments. This is why

I keep insisting inner spiritual evolution is needed, in which our own spiritual energies can undo the complex separation engendered by the mind and ego, thereby bringing them closer to oneness.

In this manner, with past and present awareness, the intellect determines whether our consciousness moves towards ego or divine awareness. Hence, consciousness is the inner perception and content of what we are. In reality, we are pure presence, beyond limited perceptions, unaware, but designed for the purpose of seeking and realizing total awareness. The mind, lured by external objects, gets swayed into accumulations of ownership via ego, choosing through dualities that which disturbs and separates the pureness of who and what we are.

We do not know our real existence unless consciousness, as the Witnessing Self, comes along and settles within our body-mind to reveal its true identity. Through self-awareness, experiences emerge and disappear, existing in duality. We perceive the outer world with our senses. But in Pure Consciousness, we become total awareness.

The sun does not know of its own existence in giving out light; like our Witnessing Self, it is singular and non-dual. In the way rays of light disclose the presence of the sun, in the same way consciousness divulges its physical presence through our perceptions. The mind, through these perceptions, dictates our initial understanding and consciousness of what we are, providing a sense of being in awareness of who we are. Therefore, awareness is *who* we are, consciousness is *what* we are, and perceptions through body-mind reflect *how* we are. Non-duality is the substratum from which consciousness comes and goes, having no independent reality. Just as we cannot exist without consciousness, awareness or absolute reality cannot exist or manifest without the body and mind.

In short, when the perceiver (awareness), perceives (through the mind) the self (subject), consciousness arises to witness what is being perceived (object). The state of absoluteness, can be reached only through awareness, hence it cannot arise in un-manifested energy. The spiritual seeker eventually realizes that there is nothing to seek since what we seek is already who and what we are.

We should keep in mind that consciousness is an indirect function of the mind; exhibiting the experiences the mind goes through, whether physical, emotional, perceptual or reflective. Another factor to be considered in understanding the concept of consciousness is that it is intrinsic and personal to the individual, being directly proportionate to one's experiences. Just as awareness manifests only in the mind, similarly, consciousness is essentially present only as self-awareness, distinct to individual existence.

Further, we need to know that one cannot exist without the other, so one's self-awareness is linked to the unified consciousness. We are all interconnected, interrelated and interdependent as one whole of *Brahman*, spirit or energy. Consciousness is a stream of experiences in awareness, centralized in the memory bank of the subconscious to experience all that is happening in the present moment. It is the centralized repository of past awareness, and thus the core processor.

In this context, it is important to point out that memory and consciousness have a strong connection. Because the 'rememberer' and the 'experiencer' are the same individual. After all, memory is nothing but impressions of our past experiences.

In order for absolute energy or *Brahman* to turn from impersonal to personal, one has to exist in self-awareness. The worldly life of dualities is as necessary as spiritual life, to realize or direct our core energy back to the cyclic path of purity. Only when an individual realizes enlightenment through complete self-surrender, which is rare, does individual consciousness merge into pure, Unified consciousness to become eternal, attaining godhood. Such enlightened souls remain in fellowship as one unified soul, like the beads of a necklace, with separate identities but strung together in unified consciousness as one.

Thus, even though reality remains permanent and changeless, shades of that reality differ as unique, remaining distinct, but joining to form the whole. Consciousness is the source of human existence, dependent on awareness. It is determined by one's individuality, through the power of reasoning. It carries the soul.

This is the reason consciousness first finds expression in self-consciousness for its distinct identity and then joins the unified consciousness. Meaning, we are part of the same absolute, impersonal energy; sustained by it; and decompose back into it. However, our psychic energy, through its experiences, retains its uniqueness or individuality, and should never be underestimated.

The subject being complex, I repeat that intelligent-energy manifests in the mind as awareness, in the form of pure spirit. This in turn witnesses the mind in making it aware and conscious. Thus, awareness settles as past awareness in the subconscious, manifesting as the content of your consciousness in the form of memory; becoming the repository, reminding us how to think and act. The moment the mind becomes conscious, it separates into dualities, to discern and choose between this and that, giving rise to ego and self-consciousness.

Consciousness is not a psychic process, neither is it a quality of the mind, it is a pure expression or substance of that Witnessing Self in total awareness.

It is the essence, being the light, which reveals all objects. There can be no thinking, feeling, willing or memory without the presence of consciousness. Through modifications from the mind, in its characterization of I-ness, conscience manifests as a finite self-consciousness, where every act of cognition is but an expression of that infinite Pure-consciousness in a mental mode.

Therefore, Self-knowledge in accordance to Advaita-Vedanta is characterized by two separate aspects; Pure infinite consciousness as the Witnessing Self and also as individual self-consciousness, which reveals the objective world. Pure-consciousness is total awareness in our limitless, spaceless universe, as the Absolute and non-dual, going beyond the subject-object relation as the Ultimate Reality.

Consciousness on interaction with the mind has three stages of evolution: the first is ignorance, when the mind is fully involved in separateness, indulging in dualities, accumulation of wealth and attachments. In this stage, the remedy is to be self-aware, to know and understand the self and if possible be guided by a self-realized guru. Self-awareness actualizes the presence of our being. It may not give us material comforts but will provide the missing link in life, filling up the emptiness we experience even in the midst of plenty. It will make us aware on what we do from moment to moment, as long as the intention is serious. This way, we may learn the actual meaning of truth, love and reality.

The second stage is self-experience, after gaining knowledge of the Self. This emphasises selflessness, compassion and non-attachment, converging in fearlessness. Knowledge is incomplete unless experienced. It is only through experience that we realize how Self-aware we are. Here, the role of the guru should end, like the doctor's after prescribing medicine. If we continue with a guru, he will preach based on his own experiences. This will be of limited use, and can even be detrimental to erasing one's own ego, as it is someone else's experiences. This depletes our psychic energies.

The third stage is God-realization or transcending to a journey of oneness, from which we have been separated. All dualities meet at a point: God/Devil, truth/untruth, good/bad, positive/negative, etc., to become One. Bliss is when one unites all duality into One absolute, non-dual as the Ultimate Reality.

This stage is extremely rare in existence and very difficult to achieve. The mind and body need to dissolve in total awareness or Pure consciousness, into oneness with the spirit. What remains is zero duality and complete self-surrender, not in nothingness or a void, but in the allness of total awareness and pure consciousness.

The ultimate purpose of any self-consciousness, in spiritualism, is to achieve bliss. Consciousness keeps wandering from one body to another, in the cycle of birth and death, experiencing pleasure and pain, until it reaches one who is Self-realized in the absolute and non-dual, uniting the mind, body and soul with the universe and the collective, cosmic consciousness of which we are all a part.

We all have a spiritual mask claiming
we are ego-less.
In fact, if there were no ego, the significance of
Consciousness would not exist.

Part II

Spiritualism claims there is only one God – the unified field of consciousness. We are a part of it and achieve fulfilment only when we Self-realize that Oneness. The Creator is thus also the Creation. In contrast, religion claims a separate God for each community, with their own beliefs, traditions and dogmas. Religion comprises three factors: cultural, ritual and spiritual. The first two are of prime importance in making us believe in a personal God of our choice. The spiritual aspect, as it always does, balances the conflicts which arise from the other two.

If and when a higher level of collective common sense prevails, the spiritual aspect will dominate and religion and spiritualism will merge into one. This, of course, seems unlikely, but we never know. Spiritualism declares, *Hari Om Tat Sat*, meaning the creator is the creation. The manifest and the un-manifest are not two but one; that the ultimate truth is, everything on earth is one single force or energy called spirit or *Brahman*.

Allow me to elaborate on a thought: 'In the gap between spirituality and religion, lies the existence of both God and the Devil.' Animals do not think, discriminate or choose; they possess limited, spontaneous awareness, linked to mere survival. However, man has been blessed with a mind which can think, discriminate, choose and also be conscious of what he is thinking, with unlimited awareness. He needs to discern and choose what he desires. This process creates a separation in the oneness of any form of energy, breaking it into duality. This is done solely by the human mind.

The mind, in order to exist, thinks in dichotomies, choosing what suits it and its body consciousness; defined as ego. The energy gets separated into opposites or dualities through the self-interest of the thinker. It is this separateness of energy which is the cause of conflicts in the mind; especially when a situation does not suit us. Perceptual thoughts, leading to anxiety, despair, suffering, etc., crop up. For, if there is happiness, sadness is bound to follow.

To balance this, we have been blessed with cosmic energy in the form of awareness, manifesting as consciousness. Thoughts triggered by external perceptions provide us with ample energy to fulfil material ambitions based on self-attachment. However, while fulfilling our desires for accumulation and sentiment, and travelling the bumpy road of positivity and negativity in good, bad and ugly situations, life is still incomplete and there is a sinking feeling or a vacuum within, which needs attention from a different level of the mind.

This is when spiritualism enters through self-awareness to awaken our individuality and create a bridge across this abyss. How we get to the other side is the strength of spiritualism. It can only be done by raising our level of awareness and cleansing our consciousness. We realize the play of duality in life. We reach the edge of the abyss, in misery and suffering, and it is there when we need to make up our mind where to go for fulfilment.

We need to bring the separated energies of duality back to their centre, as close as possible to where they parted ways. We need to accept every duality with equal grace and respect, without discrimination. The methodology has been explained in greater detail, in Book III, *The Ultimate Reality*. Consciousness remains as individual conscience, depending on the degree of awareness manifesting in the individual, until he Self-experiences and realizes the reality of his true being.

While matter can be found in different shapes and forms of energy, psychic energy has uniquely different characteristics. The mind functions in different ways during different states: in the waking state we are with the world; in the sleep state we are with nature; and in the dream state we are with our deepest desires.

There can be no self-identity without individuality. In the same way, there can be no unity between two opposing identities without understanding and awareness of the differences. Moreover, for awareness to exist the opposite must prevail. What I must emphasize here is we are all unique in our individual ways. We exist in the mind, within ourselves; separating our energies through duality and thus remain ignorant and incomplete. We can achieve completeness only when we, individually, realize the meaning of oneness, not through self-interest but in self-surrender and acceptance of our ego.

I repeat: we are all part of the same absolute energy in body, mind and soul; sustained by this energy; and finally return to the universal energy, which is one unified force, absolute and non-dual. Every element is a part of the same absolute content, in continuum. We were separated from it through our perceptions, but never disconnected.

Allow me to elaborate the same with another scientific phenomenon. The randomness of thoughts into dualities is similar to the fundamental law in nature i.e. the law of thermodynamics, expressed by entropy. The law clarifies that in any system which is not in a state of equilibrium, entropy or disorder will increase until the system ultimately revives its state of equilibrium. Similarly, Pure Consciousness is equilibrium in its absolute state, which on contact with the mind separates and gets modified into ego and individual self-conscience.

This disorder or its entropy, keeps increasing in chaos and disorder in proportion to the degree of duality. The same keeps incessantly evolving spiritually with love, selflessness, detachment, gratitude and compassion in order to return to its absolute equilibrium, from where it parted.

Therefore, as we exist in duality, be alert and watchful of the mind and its environment. Observe and be aware; restrict choices in order to understand, indulge in acceptance to outgrow and transform the self for greater fulfilment. Create a balance or centre through awareness of our real presence, from one moment to the next in mindfulness. This is our role in life, which will engender less fear and anxiety and provide a greater sense of freedom. Separation of the self into dualities is the cause of all suffering.

To practice spiritualism is to go beyond thoughts of a separated mind towards that centre of Oneness, in order to witness who, what and how we really are. Personally, I try to live by witnessing my thoughts and going with the flow; accepting both positive and negative with equal grace and respect; concerned with the how and why of what I am doing in this existence rather than its outcome.

My desire demands; comfort, sex and ego.
My intellect decides to reason.
My awareness cries for unconditional love.
My consciousness determines what I really want.

Chapter 9
Sex, Love & Spirituality

Normally, when we think of love with a partner, sex seems inherent. The composition of love is so wide and its place in the human life so supreme that it is commonly said that, 'God is Love'. Here, we will restrict the discussion to the relationship between love and sex and its effect on our mind, body and soul.

There are so many misleading beliefs about sex and love that it becomes necessary to untangle them first and then go on to explore how the communion between sex and spirit is so intimately connected. The oldest known religion in the world, Hinduism, has always regarded sex at a spiritual level. Unlike Christianity, Hinduism (and spiritualism) does not preclude sex. In fact, enforced celibacy goes directly against the soul of any being.

Many ancient monuments and temples, like Khajuraho, Puri and Konark, have erotic sculptures engraved all over them. Hindu scriptures, going back thousands of years, from *tantra* to the *Vedas,* hold sex or *kama* (sexual desire), to be one of the four main requisites in life; the other three being, *dharma* (righteousness), *artha* (economic prosperity) and *moksha* (liberation).

Today, we wonder at such a public display of eroticism in the sculptures on temples, which would no longer be permitted. This is rather ironic in an age of sexual explicitness and sexual violence. In these temples, there exists an atmosphere of calm and sacredness. They were erected and thus decorated for the purpose of shedding lust. When we look at them meditatively, we begin to understand the depth of sex, as a source of unlimited energy.

Thus we must first expunge the idea from the

mind that sex is evil, dirty, damaging to self-esteem, and cannot be discussed openly. Only then will our thoughts transform to a higher spiritual level on the subject of sexual energy. Most subjects have their gross, subtle and core effects on the objective self; revealing the mental and spiritual essence which finds reflection in the body and mind.

When we look at the physical aspect, then yes, sex is purely related to pleasure and reproduction. Bodies meet to conjoin in bodily love and fall in love with lust. The focus is on two bodies coming together to release sexual energy mechanically and conditionally. This is where all the misconception about sex begins.

Then there is the mental or psychological level, where love goes beyond physical sex to create a bond of security, companionship, familyhood and social obligation – holding two people together. In this case, both the mind and body are involved, but conditionality remains. Such love also has physical, mental, social and economic conditions, involving expectations from one another.

Here, the mind plays the most important role. But the problem with the mind is that thoughts and emotions are never stable; they keep changing from one circumstance to another, depending on our wants and expectations. For example, so long as the mind does not possess the desired one, we are obsessed with that person. But after marrying the person we have mentally and emotionally loved, we begin to take the person for granted. Very soon, our eyes and mind wander and attraction for others grows within us. We start fantasizing and the sexual hunger within us increases – all because of the erratic mind. In both the above cases, love is given in exchange for something. It is separated in duality and is thus incomplete.

The third type of love is at the spiritual level. It has been highly spoken of in ancient studies. In spirituality, love is considered a spiritual domain, signifying union and oneness. In spiritualism, all that exists is the manifestation of a single spirit or energy, not two. It is the union of souls, merging in harmony, with no conditions, only awareness. Each soul is aware they are not two but one and there is no separation through expectations or duality. Each realizes the presence of the other as a compassionate being, not just as a body and mind. Spiritualism views love and sex as sacred, where two separated energies unite to become one.

This is why sex and meditation are also deeply interrelated, as both signify oneness – meditation for communion with the pervading spirit, and sex for conjoining two organisms. In both cases, we achieve oneness with the whole; the mind becomes still; there are no thoughts to disturb the purity and totality of what exists. There is only awareness and knowing that we are flowing in love and harmony.

You will notice how a woman becomes calm and serene after she has conceived, with the child existing in oneness with her, in the womb for nine months. Her urge for physical sex gradually diminishes while spiritual sex (the unconditional love for her child) awakens. Is this leaning towards the spiritual rather than the physical, absent in men? A non-spiritual man is interested in raw sex; emotional only as long as desire persists. He is like a hunter looking for prey, to boost his ego. His eyes keep wandering and seeking.

Due to a lack of understanding about the relationship between love, sex and spiritualism, both religion and sex have gone to extremes of duality. People go to one in order to forget the other, not realizing that everything is a manifestation of the same energy. What better example of this can there be than rising in spiritual sex, love and compassion, rather than falling into conditional love? This is what the ancient temples and monuments wish to portray. The more desire is suppressed, the greater will be the urge for gross sex. What is needed is awareness and meditation to understand the basis of love and sex. One should never mistake or confuse lust for love.

Sex and meditation both involve silencing and focusing the mind by centring attention on one focal point. As in orgasm, the mind becomes totally cut off from all other factors and is at its peak of concentration – the highest degree one can achieve in any form of meditation. We can also reach a stage, through spiritual awareness, when we realize that coital energy, having served its purpose, is wasted. Sexual energies, at this stage, need to be channelled upwards through certain yoga practices. Sex and spirit are interrelated due to their cosmic relationship of promoting togetherness.

Besides the spiritual effects of sex, science has discovered tremendous health and psychic benefits. Sex definitely has a feel-good factor. It is an exercise, a cardiovascular therapy which releases positive hormones such as oxytocin, endorphins, testosterone and oestrogen. It lowers stress and fosters intimacy and emotional closeness. It also makes one look younger and improves immunity levels and longevity.

Spirituality believes that sexual energy has a meditative effect, dissolving desire through awareness and enhancing the energy of life by transmuting our energies through breath. When sex is pure and not merely physical, it signifies that two bodies are essentially one. The separated energies of the male and female halves combine as a single energy, coming closer to their oneness.

It is normal to think of unity only when there is disorder and strive for equilibrium while living in such duality. Sexual energy is one of the most powerful human energies, combining physical, mental and emotional aspects to derive unity. Spiritualism seeks to move this energy from the lower *chakra* to the mind *chakra*.

The transmutation of reproductive energy into a sublime force through awareness, which otherwise would be wasted in excessive sexual activity, can create a new life for us. Let me try to explain this in another way: when a boy grows into a youth, sex enters his thoughts and a lot of energy is wasted in dreaming, thinking and acting. But, as he matures and reaches the ages between 30 and 40, much of that sexual energy is transmuted to his brain and used to further his life goals.

Love and compassion are divine. Compassion is the higher awareness of oneness which spirituality requires and is essential for the journey toward fulfilment. Selflessness and compassion go hand-in-hand in experiencing God. All enlightened or realized souls use compassion as the basis of communion with others. Compassion is the indicator of the maturity of our emotions. If we practice it sincerely, it leads to self-fulfilment. The other extreme of compassion is sorrow, misery and indifference.

For self-development, it is necessary to consider humility and selflessness to be major components of equanimity. The journey begins with unconditional love. Selflessness leads us towards fearlessness. Godliness is the ideal path to our ultimate destination, Oneness. All these methods are the means to balance our lives and give back to society in return for all that we have received.

Love is the emotion necessary for internal purification. It dissolves all negative emotions. Throughout history people have believed that love comes from the heart rather than the mind. The heart and brain, in order to function in balance, have to be in constant dialogue with one another. We notice our heart rate and pulse changing with every emotion, revealing how they are connected by the nervous system.

Love has two connotations: one is relative – a relationship between two human beings, signifying expectations, possessiveness, attachments, desires, demands, jealousy, etc.; and having as its opposite, hatred. The other form of love is its spiritual absolute – pure, unconditional and serene; an antidote to everything negative the mind perceives or conceives. Love in either form, besides the fulfilment it confers, is also the supreme healing power. The ability to erase and neutralize all negativity makes this energy paramount and divine. Love in its non-dual and absolute form, demands complete sacrifice and self-surrender. It thus remains eternal.

On the other hand, when expectations arise from love and remain unfulfilled, it creates hurt, contempt and hate, turning love into its opposite. We need to accept both dual and non-dual love, as we cannot do without either; while keeping the mind aware and non-attached as much as possible. When pure and pristine love flows, it dissolves all negativity it touches.

Love moves slowly, its opposite, fear, moves quickly. For example, it may take years to gather a group of people who think and feel as you do about love. But the same group can be gathered in no time, if we express hatred for a cause, person, group or society.

Love is the presence of truth and compassion, whereas hate thrives on greed and fear. This is while our spirit flourishes in love the mind is focussed on self-centredness. Love is spontaneous and an experience of the now. When the mind captures it to understand and narrate the experience, it no longer remains the same.

Love, converted into thoughts and feelings, creates expectations, conditions, preferences, possessiveness, jealousy, etc., so try to experience love less through the perceptual or cognitive mind and more in its spiritual form. That is where love attains purity.

Lust and possessiveness are often mistaken by the mind for love. The cognitive mind confuses love, after it experiences it, and love no longer retains its totality. Such love gets separated into mixed feelings and thoughts of this and that. Love cannot be taught, described or narrated by the mind. That is why the mind can never rise in love, only fall. Love requires knowing and awareness of the harmony within, in order to be experienced and realized.

The gist of this chapter with respect to sex and love, tries to convey that the conformity between the two, between man and a woman should transform from physical to psychological in family-hood, eventually evolving in to the realm of spirituality. Where we live and die for the other, rather than harbouring feelings of expectations and possessiveness. Love in its essence means giving freedom to each other.

The beauty of love is that it is the only energy that fulfils on being given as well as by being received. Love has no ego. It is unconditional. It is neither related to the heart, the emotions nor one's perception. It is pure experiential energy. We cannot pursue love. It exists within us, without us even knowing. It flows spontaneously through giving, whether to an individual in passion or as togetherness in compassion. Love can only be experienced in silence, not through words.

When the mind is ignorant; awaken it.
When the mind wanders; quieten it.
When the mind is chattering; still it.

Chapter 10
The Mind & Us

Humans alone have minds and hence a pre-eminence over other living creatures. The body is considered gross energy, whereas the mind is subtle energy, with consciousness at its core. The mind, not being physical, can neither be measured nor seen; nor does it require space to exist. The study of the mind is perhaps the most complex and baffling of all subjects. Science has no concrete answers with respect to many aspects in the functioning of the mind, especially its link to experiencing and consciousness.

Even if one were to ask an average person what the mind is, he would most likely identify it as personality, the self, or being, rather than the brain. Yet the scientific world is convinced that the human mind is a bundle of electrochemical activity inside the brain. Whether consciousness is a separate entity than the perceptual brain, remains unanswered.

While philosophy and science continue to wrestle with understanding the mind, what we definitely know is that an individual's personality is the direct result of the physical, emotional, intellectual, psychological, financial and spiritual state, which determines the quality of his objectives, subjectively, during his life. Since the mind has always baffled science, let us go to its spiritual aspect, and see how spiritualism has dealt with the study of mind and matter.

Eastern spiritualists have been very clear in their understanding of the mind. To them, mind precedes matter. The individual mind is nothing but a part of universal consciousness. Wherever the mind may be located, it is in direct communion with all other minds. The sense organs assist the mind in perceiving external objects whereas consciousness is responsible for inner perceptions. Both unite to manifest in the mind as knowledge.

All knowledge is a by-product of the mind. Whatever one knows is through the mind. In any mental perception, four distinct elements are involved: the external object, the sense organ, perception, and finally the conscious-self.

The mind is a receiver of intelligence and information in the form of the impulses it receives, like antennae, from the external environment. The mind processes that data and instinctively sorts, accepts, rejects or modifies it, while acquiring further inputs from memory.

Simultaneously, the mind assesses the information for credibility, suitability and probability, through the emotions unique to each mind and the sphere of its moral, ethical and social perceptions. Between the input and output of data, there is a loss of mechanical time. As a result, thoughts are related to what has already happened. This creates a further separation between the psychic self and the reality of the now. It creates a distinction between the experiencer and reality by revealing any object/ circumstance/situation through a processed screen and a time lag.

Even though the mind performs an incredible number of simultaneous functions, there remains a tiny time difference between the input and output of data. The moment the mind becomes conscious, raw quantitative processing gets transformed into its qualitative characteristics, with texture and colour. Due to this a separation occurs between the mind as processor, and the mind as experiencer.

The experiencer, being in the now, is able to witness and be aware. It even observes how the experiencing mind starts to identify and don the mantle of ownership, using filters to discern and choose between all the acquired data, creating uncontrolled craving and desire. This sort of false ownership by the mind, forming body-consciousness is based on ego. Ego is the false representation of me and mine, believing itself separate from the real 'us'. It is thus the job of the experiencer-mind to remove all the layers of interest in self-desire that the 'other' mind accumulates.

The human mind also possesses the unique capacity to act or react by discerning, discriminating and choosing, to counter and neutralize stimuli according to individual likes and dislikes. Every stimulus, whether physical or internal, forms a unique experience in the mind. For example, different individuals experience any single colour in different shades. With billions of neural cells (neurons), a person perceptively and intuitively, using the medium of thought, forms his individuality according to his physical, intellectual, emotional and spiritual experiences.

The neural process commences in the mind with sensory perceptions collecting data. This data, via thought, undergoes an experiential process to determine what it is. The experiential process is determined by the intellect using its power of reasoning, which is the outcome of its past experiences. The intellect has the power to accept or reject any experiential inference, relying on memory. Most physical experiences manifest as knowledge from the memory bank. Inner experiences require more intervention from awareness and the intellect to form its intention.

The mind becomes aware not only of itself but through immediate awareness is conscious of what it is experiencing. Consciousness is nothing but a series of experiences, which behaves as the 'rememberer' of experiences, relying on the data in our memory. In short, consciousness is what we are.

The memory is the storehouse of all experiential data, supporting both the intellect and the inner mind. It all happens simultaneously in the mind – the intellect as our personal power or individuality, through awareness and consciousness acting as the 'rememberer', through memory. Awareness thus becomes who we are – the intelligence-energy responsible for all that happens in the mind.

The mind also receives a bonus. This occurs before the neural process can take over, through thoughts, to interpret anything. This prime, pristine, fresh intelligence-energy is what we call creativity, intuition or imagination. This is added to all that the mind receives through its antennae from the cosmic zone. These fresh and immediate flashes of awareness, in the form of intuition or imagination, occur spontaneously in the mind before they can be converted into analytical thoughts.

There are two factors which have strong influences on the mind – intellect and emotion. Even though emotion is linked to the heart, it is a direct manifestation of the mind, through thoughts playing and churning around. Emotion, in fact, hampers the ability of the intellect to take rational and unbiased decisions, becoming the cause of many problems. The intellect is the source of common sense and reasoning in deciding what is right and wrong. Emotion sways the intellect.

From its interactions with people, the environment and circumstances, the intellect undergoes a constant tussle between the thought processes of emotion and reason. This is basically the cause of all our conflicts and the reason for our dual behaviour, for happiness and sadness following each other and making life such a paradox.

The intellect is also influenced by three other factors: first, the hereditary framework of the mind; second, emotional dependence through attachments; and third, the intensity of the desires within. All three join hands for the intellect to intend and decide a course of action and so, experience.

To repeat: awareness is the source of all that happens in the mind. The intellect is the centre of reason, the base of common sense and knowledge. It arrives at the appropriate mental mode through consciousness, in order to act. All three factors of the mind merge to form one's uniqueness and individuality.

The body is the gross reflection of a person. The mind is the collector of thoughts which build personality through perception and awareness. The intellect applies reason and control to the incessant wants of our thoughts, in order to discriminate and choose between desires and consciousness.

The primary function of the mind is to fulfil one's desires based on self-interest. But the 'us' can observe and be aware, and decide to rule the mind. So, besides the body and mind, there is another element hidden within us, witnessing all that the body and thoughts are experiencing. Spiritualism refers to this witness-experiencer as the real Self, which lies beyond the thoughts generated by external perception. This witnessing Self is Pure consciousness and completely aware.

All of us have this witnessing force. It lies dormant until awakened, silently making us aware and conscious of the way we think and act. When consciousness attaches itself to objects, it dilutes its own purity by being affected by the dualities of life. To return self-consciousness to divinity is the role of spiritualism. The Self, as an experiencer in awareness, makes us conscious of totality. In fact, life is the sum total of our experiences, forming the content called consciousness.

To repeat: the real Self is the experiencer (awareness), experiencing (mental processes), through the body (object), as the experienced. Therefore, in making us aware and conscious of any experience, our awareness forms the experience. The mind takes the role of experiencing while the body, as the object, becomes the experienced. Awareness becomes the context of the real self and consciousness becomes the content. The simple reason being – awareness comes before consciousness.

For this reason, science has not been able to solve the mystery of consciousness. Science deals with the study of objects, through its theory of reductionism; not in totality. When confronted with a subject like that of the Universe and unified consciousness, being one, science can only refer to it as dark energy.

While the mind experiences any object, using intellect and data collected in the memory along with perceptive thoughts to decide between this and that, it experiences waves of turbulence and conflict due to emotional reactions to stimuli. Awareness, witnessing all this, tries to guide the experiencing mind by making it conscious of what it is doing.

This is where spiritualism enters to awaken the spirit, the divine, within us. Through yoga and meditation, we can quieten and transform the mind, moving from body-consciousness to awareness of divine-consciousness, through experiential realization. We are not just the body and the mind, but a continuum of the unified consciousness comprising the whole Universe.

Spiritualism believes the mind is the wall between us and God. The mind focuses on our desires and separates us from the awareness and divinity, which unites. Awareness balances the external thoughts designed for self-interest by the ego, replacing them with spontaneous thoughts and intuition, which are our saviours.

Since the mind is biased towards outer perceptions due to our existence in duality, an individual is bound to self-interest, desires and emotional attachments, in a vicious cycle of pleasure and pain. In such a case, we are the victims and the mind is the ruler. We remain in ego-consciousness. On the other hand, if we were able to use the mind meditatively, in a state of sublime observation, alertness and awareness, there would be less of this and that, and more of the presence of the One. Be fully aware of that presence in all that exists. There is only this – one whole, complete energy which is omnipresent, omniscient and omnipotent as unified and pure consciousness, spirit, *atman* or God.

Spiritualism tells us, existence is nothing but a separation of energy or spirit, into duality, creating positive and negative illusions. Our purpose in life should be to constantly be aware of every unit of life and experience. Accept both extremes of dualities – positive/negative, happiness/sadness – with respect, bringing them as close to their centre as possible, back to the oneness from which they came. They are not two, simply different sides of the same coin. We have God on one side as Pure consciousness and the Devil as desires and ego on another. If God is there to bless us, the Devil resides on the other side to make us miserable. One is part of the other. But if we accept both with awareness and grace, we will be in a better position to outgrow and transform these experiences.

The mind, functioning with self-serving objectivities, is ignorant and needs to be awakened and balanced through awareness and consciousness. The mind, in fact, survives and thrives on ego, inviting conflicts, mental disturbances and disharmony, because it functions only through self-interest, to satiate its desires at any cost. Completeness and fullness can only be achieved through a conjunction of worldly and spiritual living.

We need to understand the Self as being the real 'us' within the mind. The Self is the pure witnessing soul, observing and making the mind and body aware and conscious of how the mind behaves; and what we should do to overcome any unfavourable situation which is causing us grief. Thoughts describing any experience have to first go into the past and relate to individual experience, which may or may not be the complete truth.

The aware Self is the subjective 'us', unrestricted by time or space. It forms our self-awareness in the subconscious mind, becoming a part of our memory, part of the sum total of our experiences in awareness. This real 'us' is life, leading the body and mind through a series of experiences. Thoughts are nothing but a part of any experience, linking our subjective mind to the objective, in order to interpret or narrate any experience. The mind reflects through thoughts but is illumined by consciousness.

That is why science, limited by objectivity and physicality, constantly revises its results, searching for truth and reality. But in spiritualism, truth remains the same forever – where truth cannot be observed, only experienced – which only happens in the now.

On the other hand, we should remember that the mind is all we have to name, define and express spirit, God, consciousness, soul, etc. It is the mind which modifies absolute awareness by its manifestation, diluting the same into self-consciousness. Moreover, it is our mind which ultimately chooses the path – physical, spiritual or both, that we follow, based upon our self-consciousness/individuality/personality; it is responsible for deciding both external and internal perceptions. Consciousness or the universe cannot exist without a perceiver to perceive and observe its reality.

The dance of the cosmos that we see and observe, is simply a play of the observable reality which our mind chooses; either the physical reality of space and time or the existential reality of now. The process commences with our basic instinct followed with imagination, intellect and intention in how to transcend from the physicality or objective self into the spirituality Self (spirit) being the subject of our life.

To sum it up, the mind is a combined sum of desire, ego, consciousness, attachments and awareness of all that we can perceive and conceive into reality. Whether we realize the togetherness in balance between the worldly and the spiritual, the material reality and the immutable, ephemeral or the eternal, visionary or the realistic; all are attributed to the mind, because it is all that we have to observe and comprehend.

These experiences differ from person to person. All I can say is, after the external and internal make up of your mind having decided on what course of action to take, ignore the rest of the chattering by the mind and focus inwards in mindfulness, into your witnessing Self, on what you intend.

Throwing away money on eating,
drinking and dressing.
Proving to others we are somebody is such a waste.
When there is so much more to realize in life.

Chapter 11
Philosophy of Money
Part I

If asked, is money good or evil, there is a tendency to spontaneously answer that it is evil. As societies have become more sophisticated, the concept of money has changed from mere exchangeability to everything being valued in terms of money. Since money is so misused, with greedy people taking to shortcuts of all types to earn more and more, it becomes quite convenient to put the blame for all evil, onto money.

Man makes money and money makes the man. For better or worse, it affects every aspect of our lives: mental, physical, social, moral, status, respect, etc. Philosophers, psychologists, politicians, religious and spiritual leaders all write and talk about the perils of money. It is cursed more than it is lauded. As income disparities widen, a large section of society remains deprived. We continue to see extreme poverty and hunger in poor countries.

In these materialistic times, a man is judged more by his net worth than who he really is. Money plays a central role, influencing his outer and inner worlds. Money has become ubiquitous, the ultimate tool required by mankind to survive. Money has almost become as vital to us as air or water – central to our happiness. Isn't it a shame that so many of us, instead of respecting money, curse it as evil?

Money is such a subject. If you have plenty, you will be condemned as well as envied. Money is so much like the mind; both are instruments to be directed by our awareness and the witnessing Self, but it turns out that both use us. Suppose, if you have too much of money, what we notice is, it brings in guilt. Your sanity starts to compare sub-consciously with all others who don't have, and out of that guilt most moneyed people start to donate and spend on charitable purposes, after years of snatching and clinging possessively to this medium with passion and greed.

It is common today, especially in developing and under-developed countries, where millions live in poverty, facing hunger, there are the few who amass unlimited wealth, often from dubious sources. In contrast, the common man works for money not by choice but under compulsion.

In the daily course of living, one is burdened by bribes and corruption not by choice but by having to succumb under pressure. Laws are rampantly broken by the wealthy, in connivance with those who rule, creating an unnecessary burden on the middle class while crushing the poor.

Moreover, cheats are protected and rewarded since there is no accountability for wrongful gain. But even here, money cannot to be blamed or considered wrong; those who control it are the cause of the evil. Money, per se, remains a detached medium despite the often dubious manner of its earning. Wrong actions slow the progress of society and the country, driving it towards its own destruction.

How can money be the cause of evil when it is the creation and product of man's effort and work? It will always remain an effect. Any 'evil' originates from man's intentions and the way a man uses his money. Anyone who has earned money the right way respects it; the man who damns money is either incapable of earning or has acquired it dishonourably.

I support George Bernard Shaw's comment on

money, 'Lack of money is the root of all evil.' Wealth is generated by effort. I would consider that man moral and honest, who awakens this ability within him. To earn money requires intelligence, determination and effort.

The ability to make money differs in each of us, because of time, circumstances and the zeal within. Hard work results in deserved rewards. The belief that money is bad mainly comes from religious and spiritual preaching. Those who do not have enough or yearn for it but fail to acquire money, take pleasure in thinking and stating, they are not subjected to this 'evil'.

It is greed that has made money such an evil. There is no doubt that the lure of money is so powerful it can rule us, unless we assert control over ourselves. The greed we witnessed recently, during the global financial crisis, is an example of this – how a few banks or men, because of their desire for abnormal profits, created a chain reaction that brought the world to the brink of economic collapse.

It is also commonly stated that money can buy comforts but not happiness. Happiness is a state of mind, one can be happy with or without money. However, surveys on happy people have shown that in the list of things that make one happy, the centuries' old saying comes true – health comes first, then wealth, and then wisdom. These factors are required to live a happier life.

Those who understand and control their money, attain purpose in life. After achieving the basics in terms of food, clothing, shelter and comforts; the wise go towards finding balance through self-actualization. They take care of interpersonal relationships and seek more balance between their exterior and inner selves.

Others are caught in the vicious cycle of profit and loss, desiring power and fame, wanting much more than they can consume. They remain ignorant and unfulfilled with their never-ending wants. Why therefore, do we keep blaming money? An excess of anything is bad for us. The way we need to find the right balance between mind, body and spirit, we also need to find the right balance in the case of money. We have to learn to use this versatile and essential tool and thereby, make our lives and others' happier.

Money is a powerful instrument; it allows us to do almost anything. It makes it easier for us to satisfy most of our desires. However, it remains only a medium; you are the navigator who has to direct this tool. You can go in any direction, good, bad or ugly, as per your choice and capacity. Certainly, anything this powerful can also be dangerous, especially in the wrong hands. Like the Internet, which has revolutionized information and communication, but which can also be highly dangerous, if misused.

The material world, dominated by money and created by man, stands in stark contrast to the internal intrinsic world of awareness or consciousness. We need to realize the significance of going beyond our ego-driven 'I, me and mine'. This awareness makes us realize that mere accumulation of wealth is not the answer to live effectively and to blossom into one's potential. There are people like Bill Gates and Warren Buffet who give back to the world and society as much as they can. Hindus consider this the ultimate in yogic practice, called Bhakti yoga. This is what I would consider as being and living rich.

Man makes money, and money makes the man.

Part II

One keeps wondering why it is a prevalent idea that money is made by the strong at the expense of the weak. Why do a fraction of people succeed in making and keeping their money while the majority struggles? Why is there such unequal distribution of money? Why do we often hear that 'money talks'? Why is it that those who have money show-off, swagger and indulge in wasteful consumption? We read all sorts of negative things about money, yet all of us are drawn to it.

One wonders why so much wealth has accumulated in so few hands, even when we are all living in the same environment and under similar circumstances. This is when philosophy and psychology becomes relevant. In our times, money is no longer simply a quantitative factor; it has a qualitative influence on our lives, as it has become the basis for survival. A collective effort is required by all, but especially by those who control money, directly or otherwise, for this disparity or inequality to diminish in times to come.

Major institutions all over the globe exercise their authority to keep the common man insecure and dependent. For centuries, rulers have been criticizing money unnecessarily, not directly to the accumulators of dirty money, because these people are invariably big donors to the same institutions, but to the have-nots, when they require them for votes, etc.

Religious and spiritual leaders, educational institutions and politicians, are all responsible for degrading this ultimate determinant. For them, money is evil. Even the Bible, in its New Testament, Timothy 6:10, has a saying, 'For the love of money is the root of all evil'. Those who preach to the masses in the areas of religion, spiritualism or socialism invariably propound that the love of money can bring about degradation in one's character.

One should remember that none of us were born dishonest; our circumstances may make us dishonest. The common man needs guidance, both for earning money and for staying honest. This is why most of us have lost the power of money, as well as the respect that we should have had for a simple word, 'profit'. We have forgotten how noble money really is.

We are learning even more corrupt practices; we accumulate and disrespect the most important means of social mobility given to us. We do not realize how it becomes not only the means but also the end in many ways, because of its strong interplay with our daily interests, attitudes, aspirations, and moral values. In fact, we need to be taught how to create, preserve, respect and use money in the manner that it deserves.

We all know that aside from the looters, fraudsters and cheaters, there are also those few who treat money with the highest esteem. They learn while they make and spend money, how to improve their lifestyle, irrespective of who says what. Always remember, money serves those who can match it the right way. Therefore, it is for us to decide and understand the meaning of 'live rich or die rich'. Money demands of us the highest efforts in courage, determination, ability, self-esteem and moral sense. Only then would we know how to make, keep and spend money and of course defend it. This is what I mean by living rich.

Religious societies, corporations, financial institutions, governments, and those who make money through looting, harbouring criminals or protecting terrorists in the name of religion, cannot expect their men to retain good moral conduct. Evil thoughts of money are bound to flourish, destroy and further widen this gap between the haves and the have-nots.

We are responsible for bringing about the proper distribution of wealth in our society in such a manner that the gap is not as wide as it is today.

Man is judged more by his net worth than who he really is.

Part III

Money, money, money! Is it the greatest wonder on earth? Indeed, it is a wonder, that even after so many examples of improper and crooked attempts at accumulating money; which have brought so much damage and suffering to the world, everyone is still eager to make even more money. This shows its immense power over us. Money is so alluring that it breeds greed in everyone, sinner or saint.

If we ask anyone, what is the most important thing in life? Normally, the answer would be: health, happiness, knowledge, love, money, etc. Money usually does not appear as the top priority, despite the fact that to balance all the above, money is the main requisite. Alternatively, money can buy food, but fails to create appetite; it may buy us the most expensive bed, but cannot bequeath sound sleep.

Market forces, through the power of money, influence the government, judiciary, our security, domestic and foreign policies and even our health. There is no way out. We are dependent on this medium in myriad ways. No one knows when and where to draw the line. Because of limitless individual wealth, a small section of society is becoming more and more affluent, whereas others are slipping into poverty.

In the broader sense, however, making money is positive and ethical. This is not considering what we inherit, or are given with no effort involved. In making money, the cycle of life moves, providing us with food, clothing and shelter. As we know, the world is not a perfect place; there are all sorts of people making money in all sorts of ways. There are many books and sites which offer techniques for making money. Let's take a look philosophically, at the essential parameters of making money and their relevance to the world today.

Great achievers have always possessed dreams and vision. Such dreams have taken those people to astronomical heights, because they believed and were convinced they could. They programmed their mind for excellence, which in turn generated abundant wealth for them. Therefore, we are not to run after money, it should follow our creative deeds and actions. Mere dreaming without applying your intelligence is exactly like what I read a long time ago – 'Living in a fool's paradise is great fun until the rent becomes due.' Therefore, if we can dream, think and act intelligently, in spite of all or any competition, there are always abundant opportunities for making money.

Secondly, we have some people who are simply creative, they do not train themselves to think as they do and often don't even know they are different. The question arises whether creativity is inborn or one can obtain it, in the process of building wealth. Fortune magazine polls showed Apple to be one of the most valuable companies in the world, with huge profits and cash reserves. We also know that Apple makes money through creativity in design, technology and operations, more than any other company does. Creativity is the main ingredient in making this company one of the most profitable in the world today.

Third, it is often said, the more we run after something, the further it runs away from us. I believe the same holds good for money. An obsession with money is not the answer. If one is dedicated and devoted to one's dream, vision, ambitions, and creativity, as long as these don't diminish, money is bound to follow. Therefore, it becomes imperative that in the art of making money, instead of us chasing it, money should follow us. At the same time, one should be careful in making and managing money, because the feeling always remains of never having enough. Our fears and insecurities tell us that we need more and more. We are afraid to look inside ourselves and face the truth – the realization that happiness comes only from living a full life.

Eastern spiritualism, realizing the relevance and significance of sex and money, understood that the mind is primarily designed for self-interest. The Vedas postulated four specific requisites in life, which even though they are as relevant today as in ancient times, are not spoken about by any moral institute or spiritual gurus. These, arranged in ascending order, are: *dharma, artha, kama,* and *moksha*. Through righteousness attain economic prosperity, fulfil sensuous desires and then consider liberation or *moksha*.

It is curiosity, which takes us towards God.
It is awareness, which draws us nearer God.
It is devotion that makes us realize God.

Chapter 12
Who is God?

God, as I see him, is space, air, water, fire, earth; whatever there is in the universe. God is beauty, joy, love and everything that exists, and into which everything dissolves. God is a part of us; he is within us. We feel incomplete without him, and are dependent upon him. God may be a product of the human imagination, but when you look around, especially at the galaxy of planets whirling about in such an orderly fashion; one wonders about that Creator.

Until the age of three, we are unaware of the concepts of 'I' or 'Who is God?' Then awareness arises about existence with the emergence of 'me and mine', we start saying 'my toy' and 'my candy', etc. Everything around becomes separated into yours, or mine in contradiction to the totality in which we live. Our parents, teachers, preachers and many others provide us an identity, name, religion, language and a big list of do's and don'ts to build our initial persona on the guidelines specified by the society or community we live in.

We are taught about a separate God to believe in and pray to during times of need and fear and to thank Him for all that He has given us. The truths we believe about existence revolve around what has been told to us that change as and when circumstances and the environment demand. Also, the process of influencing or imposing on us continues by preachers and gurus, based on their version of religion and faith. Thus man has always lived by faith in whatever the mind believes.

However, the times are changing; a modern man, with a wider perspective and a better education, is different. He questions everything; wishes to know the truth behind existence, its purpose and meaning and the presence of the Almighty. If God is indeed the imagined projection of mankind, what is the reality of our presence in the form of body, mind and soul? This must be the reason Buddhism is so attractive to the modernity of our thought today. It avoids the word 'God' and considers our existence to be illusory in this world of desires and attachments.

Today, 'Spiritual but not religious' has become a popular phrase to signify those who do not accept traditional organized religion for furthering their inner growth. SBNR today is mostly prominent in the United States, where as per survey over 25% of the population today identify more to this term than any other demographic region in the world. SBNR is gaining popularity with evolving new-age spiritualism, where the reference to God is more towards a higher power or in transcendent nature of reality with no-connection towards any religious affiliation or affirmation.

On the other hand, the mind has been conditioned to such an extent that whatever one may say; an atheist, even if he claims about his disbelief in religion is confused. So strong has been the conditioning of religion over centuries and generations, in spite of your mind refusing to believe, you come out inadvertently without realizing in support of the religion and its community that you live and are surrounded with. Both however add up to belief in a Higher Power of some kind.

We have an interesting quote given by Buddha: *Believe nothing, no matter where you read it, or who said it, no matter if I have said it, unless it agrees with your own reason and your own common sense.* Signifying the relevance of how important it is to base your inner convictions on what your inner sense through experience will tell you, rather than through what you blindly believe and understand from others, irrespective of belief in God or in yourself.

It is in the quest to getting such subtle answers that we realize our personal sense of self ultimately has to surrender to the presence of the Universe, time and time again. A sense of surety arises about the existence of that silent unified Oneness, where the small presence of 'I-ness' reveals the 'Allness' of that timeless, limitless presence.

Existence bows to the expression of life. One starts to understand the reality behind existence within the context of the subject of who the doer really is. The ultimate reality, behind Oneness versus separation and omnipresence versus nothingness or emptiness becomes clearer.

Transcendental reality expresses itself as the subject of that unified consciousness connecting to the state of self-awareness to which we belong. Where, consciousness/awareness becomes the subject of who we are. It is the core of our being, revealing its presence in the emergence of the object of existence in the form of body and mind.

Science is coming very close to what the mystics have been saying for centuries, in proving that the reality behind mind, matter and spirit emerges from a single source. Quantum physicists describe the Universe as energy, which can neither be created nor destroyed. Is this the oneness that modern physics and mystics relate to?

Mystics claim that all that exists is but a manifestation of one spirit called *Brahman*; when in absolute form, the spirit is self-realized as God and in separation into dualities. We are a part of God in the same content and quality.

Science postulates the force that sustains the subatomic waves and particles of energy of which matter is made, is composed of an organized or condensed energy in slow vibration. Not only are there quantum leaps in the subatomic field of energy, we find the same leap by the unified awareness/ consciousness in the advancement of an individual or a society.

In a similar manner, spiritualism claims that all avatars and supernatural humans who have ever existed on Earth and have been conferred the title of God are none other than the absolute content of this organized energy. Consciousness in a man thrives as ego, till he remains separated. But the same consciousness also has the capacity of God-realization.

The Big Bang is a scientific theory by Professor Stephen Hawking who says it is not necessary that God created the universe – 'Because there is a law such as gravity, the universe can and will create itself from nothing. Spontaneous creation is the reason there is something rather than nothing, why the universe exists, why we exist.'

Therefore, we cannot define 'nothing' as empty. As per the laws of physics, nothing or even a vacuum is full of the force of potential and kinetic energy. It is so much like the concept of *Brahman* enfolding all that exists, being nothing, and this nothing, being everything in which all exists. Nothingness or the 'void' which is considered empty, is a misnomer. A 'no mind zone' in meditation does not literally empty the mind, but replaces confusion with awareness, towards selflessness, compassion and non-attachment.

Mystics also concluded that we are none other than the creator or God himself. '*Tat Tvam Asi*': 'Thou art That' or 'I am That'. They all mean the same thing – that 'I' am God. The mystics explain that the Creator is the creation. We are a part of that, and we possess the same quality as God. The reason being that both the subject (God) and the object (us) have the same absolute energy as the basic constituent. Our consciousness transmigrates from one cycle of birth and death to another in order to revive the separated energies of dualities back to their oneness into absolute, in order to reach that totality in completion or God-realization.

According to the theory of cause and effect, we notice that the effect takes place only at an emotional energy level, due to our likes and dislikes, which only arise through self-interest. However, the major part of our mind, the cause being the subconscious, remains unaffected. Likewise in an ocean, waves keep forming and breaking, but the expanse of the ocean remains unchanged. Since only the effect changes, with the cause remaining the same, it can be concluded that the individual, emotional and egoist changes in our mind are but temporary, being illusory, apparent and unreal.

The real part of our mind is in the subconscious where the infinite, limitless, non-dual, pure energy, which is absolute, having no relativity or duality, resides in the form of spiritual awareness. This is where our divine presence, or God, exists, as the Witnessing Self. Therefore, an external or separate God for each religion is the product of our imagination and an expression of the human mind only. It is purely up to us now, how we perceive or conceive of Him, since science or technology has no answer for such enquiry. Religion has three aspects, cultural, ritual and spiritual. It is only when religion matures into the third level of spiritual practice that they merge into one, in unity with one God for all.

It is the Absolute or the subject from which the object or the relative content arises for the mind to infer anything. Similarly, from the Absolute or from the field of unified consciousness comes the experience of self-awareness. When this attaches to any object say the mind, it modifies the same into self-consciousness to undergo the experience of material content in duality in order to experience what we call as existence.

Therefore, awareness emerges first, in order to make the mind aware to be conscious of an object. In the subject-object relationship, awareness remains aloof and is not part of the consciousness playing its dual role within the mind. This is how God is referred to; in total awareness we are God and in self-consciousness or ego, we are but an object in mind and body as matter.

We can live by faith, belief or ignorance and still perceive God as a person, in some form or the other. The mind needs data from the sense organs to define an entity. If we cannot see, feel, touch, taste or hear God, then how can He be defined? We cannot only relate to God through words and images.

God can only be experienced in awareness. We will discover God in awareness of compassion, selflessness and non-attachment in existential living. He reveals himself as the witnessing Self in each one of us, but we listen more to our ego than the subtle God within us. If only man could realize this awareness, rather than try to turn God into a definable entity...

Through this ignorance, religions overpowered the world, influencing and dominating their respective civilizations and making sure of the ascendency of their values and philosophies. They had their own version of the truth and reality, and these philosophical attitudes formed the basic structure of the development of society and government.

For millennia, we presumed that matter and energy were two separate entities. Nobody would reconcile to the ancient idea postulated by spiritualism that a human being could be an abstract field of consciousness in the form of energy and spirit, where body and mind existed only as apparent reality, until

Albert Einstein and a few other scientists clarified that mind, body and matter all comprised one entity as a whole, which was both physical and spiritual – form and formless were one.

Theologians may dislike the idea of Oneness, and also that all Gods are one. However, they need to realize, that the heart and end of each faith meet at the same point. It is only abstruse minds which propagate separations, for their own fame and purpose.

Whether it is the Big Bang theory, *Brahman* or Tao, they all claim, nothing is not empty but full. Some call it 'nothingness' and the other, 'nothing'. Even in a vacuum, there is a force of energy. All forms, in order to exist are merely separated aspects of the same reality, functioning in a paradox, dualities or opposites. They all coexist as a manifestation of undivided oneness in continuum, in which God Himself becomes a part of that existence in total awareness.

The phenomenon which physicists are drawing closer to is that what we perceive as empty is but infinite dark energy. The experiencer and the experienced, the knower and the known have all arisen from but one field, one source; which we humans have named energy or spirit, where the mind plays the role of a processor in experiencing and knowing all there is to know.

Do we really need God? Yes! When the mind plays its perceptual role in states of fear, desire and in seeking forgiveness – out of fear we cry for Him. But in existential living with compassion, selflessness and non-attachment as our *mantra,* we experience God moment to moment in fearlessness.

The ancient scriptures of Eastern spiritualism have revealed three main directions to experience and realize God. These paths may be different in their nature, but they all merge in their purpose of being one with the divine. They are: *Karma* yoga – selfless action; *Bhakti* yoga – devotion; and *Jnana* yoga – knowledge and wisdom. All three join in their aim to attain union with the divine in totality. The path of devotion is to surrender in compassion, the path of knowledge is to know how to realize Pure consciousness and the path of selflessness makes one fearless in what we do.

These three virtues were realized by Buddha, Jesus, Krishna and a few others. Though extremely rare and not easily realized by us, these paths definitely take us towards absolute existence in God-realization. These luminaries were not religious in any manner but were able to reach the pinnacle of consciousness in existential and experiential realization with awareness in compassion, fearlessness and non-attachment – the three yoga practices in becoming one with God.

When we see, feel or experience Him with our conscious mind, He is limited to our religion, culture, caste and creed. God here is apparent and not real; a ritual, where we remember Him mainly during times of fear, want or emotional outbursts. In this life of duality, His existence gets limited or related to the concept of the Devil on the other side.

Buddha wasn't born a Buddhist or Christ a Christian. To describe them in such a manner is simply a case of exploitation by these religions. If there were somebody there to create the Universe, it would mean that God or the religious form of God was already present. If we ask, who or where God is, people point towards the sky or the ocean. Please remember, God does not manifest himself. He is in us, with us, and around us. It is for us to become aware of His presence and divinity, deep within our subconscious mind; to experience and realize Him away from the vanities of this world.

The presence and awareness of God is inside and all around us. Individuals and thoughts may come and go, but the supreme energy in this universe will keep flowing. It is for us to learn, become aware and distinguish between the energy of the ego and the infinite, unlimited energy of God within us. The 'I' as ego consciousness is ephemeral and unreal. The 'I' derived from experiential awareness in existential living, is your reality – where God exists. The 'I' is common to both, one is projected from your ego, and the other is the Lord within us.

God is infinite and eternal. When your mind and body dissolves in this timeless, limitless and spaceless energy, you become God. In body and mind we are finite; we cannot perceive or conceive the infinite through our limited mind. The mind requires that which can be defined; God, being eternal, cannot be defined, unless the mind dissolves into the infinite.

The lonely separated spirit keeps reminding us.
Life will remain lonely, sad and discontented.
Wealth and intelligence, shall keep us ignorant and incomplete.
Until we experience and realize the Divine.

Chapter 13

Divine Presence ...
Do we really need him?

In the previous chapter, 'Who is God?' it has been upheld that God is a manifestation of the mind. It is up to us how we perceive and exercise our faith in Him, either in the form of a supernatural being, which is supposedly omnipresent, omniscient, and omnipotent or the Divine presence within ourselves, which can be experienced and realized.

As per Wikipedia, 'Hinduism is often called the oldest living religion in the world.' It seems to have originated in approximately 2500 BC. Hindu beliefs were recorded in *The Bhagavad Gita,* which revealed that the gods were subject to a supreme *Brahman* God. This is translated as 'absolute reality' meaning God and an individual are incorrectly or apparently considered two separate entities. In reality, however, 'He who knows himself to be no different from Me, is one with Me, he is wise and is liberated from birth and death.'

This presence of energy in the time-space continuum, and everything that exists within it: the consciousness of awareness of the limitless Self, is what is referred to as God. God is everything, and everything is God, meaning, the Creator is the Creation Himself.

Whether the divine presence is the awareness buried deep in us, or His conceptualization in monotheism (belief in one God), we all seem to have some faith and belief in God and depend on Him for our deeds and misdeeds.

I read in the newspapers, that 40 separate studies conducted in 20 countries have concluded that we are all inclined to believe in God and an afterlife.

These studies have suggested that religion, spiritual practices and even atheism are primal responses which spring from the basic impulses of the human mind.

In the 1990s, research by neuropsychologist Michael Persinger and neurologist V. S. Ramachandran at the University of California, led to the discovery of a 'God spot' in the human brain. This area is located in the neural connections of the temporal lobes of the brain. Scans showed that these neural areas are activated whenever the research subjects are drawn into discussions upon spiritual topics.

Even though this is no evidence of the existence of God, we do notice that the young and strong have lesser inclination than the weak and old, in seeking and embracing God. Now the question is – do we really need a divine presence?

First, let us understand who we are. It is said that we are what we think. We see and hear what we want to, as dictated by our thoughts. This thinking process is based on the past knowledge we have, and through this past, we create our reality and perception of now and project to our future.

This perceived reality then becomes manifested into, 'I, me and mine'. But have you noticed there is always another voice within us, trying to tell us what we should or should not do, ignoring the likes and dislikes of 'I, me and mine'? We might not pay attention to this subtle intelligence-energy, but it is always there.

The presence of this witnessing self within us lies forgotten. Many of us do not discover this other self, in the midst of our desire for emotional satisfaction and material comforts. On one hand we have the mind ruling us through desire, emotion and attachments of the ego, and on another, we have our witnessing self which can free us. Let us understand how a comparison between the two could help us to answer the question of why we need the presence of the divine in our lives.

Whatever we may say, the mind is the source of everything that we conceive of. It is the foundation of all knowledge. It behaves like an antenna, which receives all perceptions inner and outer, and processes and stores data in its hard disc in the form of memory. Further, it analyses and calculates and also transmits data (in our self-interest) with desire and emotions, through the medium of thought. The problem starts when we equate the mind with the Self and start to depend on whatever the mind demands. Then, instead of using the mind, the reverse happens and the mind uses us.

It is advised by many sages and great masters that one should still the mind and stop its incessant chatter. One should be in a no-mind zone, thoughtless, and devoid of words to be able to experience that divine presence. How true! But is this really possible in the world that we live in? What can we do if we do not wish to renounce it all and become like monks chanting *mantras* the whole day, trying to silence our minds?

The mind is responsible for making us human – how can we deny the presence of the mind? It is too powerful to be silenced, except in deep sleep, in a drugged state or in death. As long as your mind is dependent on external perceptions, your ego will be present and your false sense of 'I' will rule. We may introspect, contemplate or meditate; the mind with its thoughts will resume its constant chattering. The mind can only stop on its own and that too when desire, attachment or the interest shown in anything, is removed. However, as long as there is a presence of interest, desire manifests bringing along a whole lot of discrimination, choosing, duality and what not. Thoughts, of course are an automatic response to any activated perception, inner or outer.

That is why we close our eyes during meditation to restrict external perception. Our perception returns the moment the energy of interest is shown by the mind, even internally. Nothingness of the mind is just imagination, unless we dissolve our mind like Buddha did in *samadhi*, by stopping the mind in its very functioning.

Everything goes on, life continues, so should mind. Everything keeps happening and moving for good or bad. We cannot stop the motion of life or its existence, so let the mind chatter, the more we worry, the more the burdens for us to carry. Just watch and observe in alertness. Your awareness will be able to tame the mind like a trainer does a tiger. Meditation is not to still the mind for a few moments, but to be aware from one moment to the next, to watch whether your mind is behaving itself or not.

When the mind is tamed, the subtle witness in us expands; the divine comes alive. We realize we are not separate, neither from the divinity within or from the mind. The mind is purely mechanical, like a computer and we are that presence in awareness, which can observe, watch and utilize the mind.

The ancient sages who first studied spiritualism were very intelligent. They were aware of the fact that in order to reach God, for an average person, the mind had to be absent, which is not possible. For this reason, they made no attempts to explain how to silence the mind, but only to dissolve it. One is supposed to mainly watch and observe the mind in awareness, unless one wants to realize enlightenment. In the Vedas they have put forward four requisites of life: one should in righteousness, attain economic prosperity, to fulfil desires, in order to go towards the path of liberation.

Both material and spiritual aspects have to be in balance before one starts on a journey to Self-realize God. Therefore, let the mind be on its own, because in no way can the mind silence its own self, unless you force yourself to do so by drugging yourself, sleeping or temporary transcendental meditation. The mind in fact, has invented an imaginary God for each society or community in the form of a religion to suit its own purposes in making Him responsible for all that the mind does, especially things we are not proud of.

There is no such thing as good or evil. It is the mind which makes it so. These are all relative characteristics for the mind to relate, compare, choose and derive for its own interest. What is good for us may not be for another. In reality or in existence, only totality persists. To separate this totality, is the job of the mind and society, for neither can exist without insisting upon what is right or wrong.

Our existence should be in conformity with reality, which can only exist in totality. In the same manner, both the mind and the divine presence are but two sides of the same coin. Both need to be treated with grace and respect and are to be exercised in totality.

At one extreme we have the Devil and in another the God as the enlightened One. We need to bring both towards their centre in oneness, where our divine presence should reveal that 'Allness' present in Oneness, in awareness of who and what we really are.

This witnessing Self is the presence within us, which makes us aware of our own Self, beyond external thoughts. It does not change, in likes and dislikes or in our reactions. It is pure, spontaneous creative intelligence-energy, not limited by our thoughts. The awareness of this presence is the divinity within, that we all share, and who we really are.

We need Him to balance and centralize our life, without which it would be a rollercoaster. Though, we are bound to live with our ego-consciousness, because that is our 'me and mine' – a mind living for the outside world, for material comforts and attachments.

If and when we shift from our animal instincts to a spiritual dimension, in awareness of our truth, reality and self in existential living, thinking is replaced by knowing. This journey is a quantum leap from our base ego-driven state. It commences when we become aware, to experience and realize that ego should be replaced by compassion, desire with selflessness and accumulations with non-attachment.

Therefore, just as one requires an intelligence quotient (IQ) to acquire wealth and comforts to fulfil one's desires, one also requires a spiritual quotient to balance psychic and emotional outbursts and to experience and realize the presence of the Divine within. How to enlighten this pre-existing divine presence in the mind or God spot is for us to decide, experience and realize on our own.

Love is the only energy, which fulfils when we give and also when we receive.

Chapter 14
The Power of Love

Love cannot be defined but can only be experienced. It is probably nature's way of keeping us together. 'Love is blind', though it was a phrase coined by Shakespeare, research supports the view, that feelings of love, suppress activity in the areas of the brain which control critical thought.

We love mainly for the satisfaction and comfort it gives us. We love because we want to love. It is said that human beings have only two basic emotions – fear and love. Fear impels us to survive and love enables us to thrive; they have been the driving force in human history for centuries.

Love and hate are intense emotions, linked to each other. It is not possible to hate a stranger. You cannot hate someone without having loved him/her earlier. Fear and hatred always dominate love, especially as love is connected to our sensory mind where thoughts vacillate between the three. Because physical love has expectations, it gives rise to imaginary fear, and hatred can creep in at any time, if those expectations are not fulfilled. As for infatuation and lust, they are often mistaken for love.

The mind, in processing our self-identified thoughts, is genetically engineered to think and react in duality, meaning loving and hating, rational and irrational, etc. Dichotomies exist, making the mind unpredictable. Here love is more of an illusion.

Love originates spontaneously; no one can demand or influence it, whereas, hatred and fear are a mental construct. In love, your divine presence is awakened. Love does not require the mind to question or calculate, unless infatuation, lust or possessiveness is mistaken for it, which is very common. In spiritual love, there is only giving, there is no expectation; the feeling just flows without wanting anything in return. This is the law of nature, we should keep in mind, that in life, giving comes before receiving, sowing comes before reaping. That is why we revere the phrase 'Love is God'.

Love can be expressed through many dimensions. The simplest is to fall in love, meaning conjugality, lust, and possessiveness, either in social or family zones. Here, making love becomes more of a fantasy. A survey in a magazine in the UK showed that most people may initially swear undying love for each other, but in reality, they fantasize and dream about someone else while making love to their partners. We may also express love in what we do, or in doing what we love, whether it is science, music, sports, art, making money, etc.

Love has no boundaries and no expectations; it should be in its absolute form in a singular field where we are free from worldly bonds, in appreciation and devotion to the Universe and nature around us. Love, whichever direction it takes, aside from the fulfilment it confers, is also the supreme healing power; it can erase and neutralize all negativity in any form.

In my opinion, the last person whom we know on earth is our own self. This may seem ironic, especially after having read so much on personal development in these books. The reason is we constantly change, creating inner conflicts. Struggle becomes part of our life, not allowing us to be aware of who we really are.

With constant change, and the obsession with 'our, me and mine', where love and hate oscillate, such love has to be an illusion. This makes it a one-way equation, which ultimately gets reduced to self-interest. When we fail to have a clear relationship with ourselves, the truth hurts. We always try to clarify with a 'but', explaining how we were or are, right. To overcome this weakness, one must have victory over oneself, to counter the bloated and false

'I' within us. This understanding of ego arises when we start to respect both negative and positive aspects of ourselves in awareness. In this manner one begins to respect and love oneself, for what one is and not what one has.

In any relationship, what is important is not what we say or do, but who we are. Unless we have a clear understanding and love for our own self, we will be unable to love others. We will have to learn why we think and feel in the ways we do. How much are we aware of our own psyche? Are we a victim of our likes and dislikes? How much command do we have over ourselves? Meaning, is your mind using you or are you the ruler of your mind? These questions can be answered only if we are true to ourselves and know who we really are.

Since thoughts keep changing with time and space, we will notice that there is one factor, very subtle, a hidden witness inside, aside from your thoughts that remains constant, observing and correcting us time and again. It is always there, as and when we require it. We realize that we are not body and mind, because we can be aware of our mind, clearly telling us, we are someone else. This is the real inner self that we need to rise with and not fall – in love.

The mind holds the sum total of our likes and dislikes, forming memory and emotions. Thoughts are born out of experience and knowledge of the past. From the past we construct our thoughts of the future, never managing to stay in the now. It is the presence of the awareness we are, which the mind fails to capture. This process of knowing the past and the ability to look into the future while existing in the present is the secret to achieving completeness in life. The whole study of spiritualism revolves around this meditative thought process.

There are two 'I's' within us, the first is connected to our sensory perceptions, empowered mainly to think about what and how we choose, from the external factors around us. The second 'I' as already explained evolves within us with years of observing and experiencing in alertness, creating that awareness within.

We discover, beyond our sensory perceptions, personal opinions and desires – a new dimension of creativity, intuitiveness and imagination. This intuitive power gives us the choice to be proactive or reactive to situations. Through awareness, we also obtain the power to switch a particular thought process or negative thoughts on and off. Those who do not have a relationship with their witnessing 'I' become so unaware that when negative thoughts enter their mind, they churn within with those thoughts, and become victims or slaves of their own negativity, causing tremendous harm to themselves.

Many people forget that the most important relation that they should have is with their own self, and how important it is to love and enjoy one's own company. Self-love is your inner strength. It is important to create a relationship and a strong linkage within to balance your egocentric 'I', with your awareness of reality and creativity. We start accepting ourselves better, personal development improves and the best part is, we discover the wonderful partner within, making life worthwhile. Therefore, to love others, we need to first love our own self, deeply enough to be able to forgive ourselves and become responsible, with self-respect and dignity.

We are nothing, without health.
Wealth is nothing, without contentment.
Knowledge is nothing, without wisdom.
Friendship is nothing, without trust.
Happiness is nothing, without freedom.
Spiritualism is nothing, without oneness.

Chapter 15
Our Body

In all of my previous essays, I have discussed how to contemplate upon your mind and beyond, in awareness and consciousness, with the objective of achieving balance in life. Sometimes, in all this study of spiritualism, we ignore a very important fact – most of us abuse our body, instead of loving and appreciating it, as we should.

Our body is the most complicated structure in the world; it reflects the story of our lives. Life sustains intelligence and energy in the form of matter and awareness. Our present state clearly reveals how we have treated our body and the effect of the mind on us. Our body and mind interact closely and influence each other to such an extent that one becomes the expression of the other. They cannot function separately, and as elaborated below, unless we respect both equally, we can never be wholly integrated individuals.

In our journey of seeking awareness for the purpose of self-development or balance, I believe the beginning should always be from the body. The body is the temple in which our soul resides. In the famous saying attributed to Benjamin Franklin – 'healthy, wealthy and wise', first comes health, then wealth, and after that, follows wisdom.

The mystery of the Universe is that most things, which exist outside, have a presence within the body. In order to live well, we have to love, respect and accept the body as a whole. Our existence has sprung from the dust, meaning, we are a part of the very same earth, in which the divine resides and we go back into the earth again. Our body would not exist if the sun, moon, ocean, forest, rain and air were not there. Even though we are a part of the Universe, we consider our self to be separate.

Every single cell of our body has its own intelligence, to carry out its functions and coordinate with related cells. DNA, the carrier of our genetic code in these cells, encodes all the data and characteristics connected to our heredity, acquired through generations of memories and emotions. DNA makes people individuals. As is our DNA, so also is perception. From this perception, the mind handles the data and reveals its intentions, which eventually come out as actions from the body.

Today, most alternative therapies acknowledge the body-mind-spirit relationship. Yoga and meditation are good examples of how a balance and interplay between the three is required to live a wholesome life. More than the desire to live longer, aim to live well. Body intelligence is the subject that takes us onto a path of healthy and preventive living. The sad part is, the money being spent on research today focuses on curing rather than preventing diseases, mainly because profits are easier and higher, when there is imbalance and ill-health.

Our body has intelligence built into it from over millions of years of mankind's evolution. The autonomous nervous system controls many of our body functions without any conscious inputs from us, like breathing, digesting, and sleeping; it maintains balance with its own intrinsic healing abilities.

The miracle of our body intelligence is that it survives in spite of our abusing it. Further, in the mind-body relationship, research shows that bacteria, especially in the gut, can alter the brain and behaviour, meaning emotional states change with the micro biome in the body.

In addition, in relation to health, newer studies have revealed that exposure to diseases may have a huge effect on IQ or brainpower. The reason is that we use a great deal of energy in running our brains, but when affected by diseases, this energy gets diverted from the brain to where it is urgently required.

Our bodies degenerate with time and age, in spite of imbibing health supplements, antioxidants, miracle herbs or even any mental or physical exercises, or efforts to manipulate our age-related telomeres. Telomeres are segments of DNA found at the end of chromosomes and every time a cell divides, its telomere gets shorter, making the cell age gradually and eventually die.

Even with so much research, our body does degenerate with wear and tear, abuse, time, and individual genetic design. Because of heredity, certain diseases are already earmarked, and the effect on our body of the pleasures and pain we go through in life clearly certifies that if there is anything certain in life, it is death.

Today, all we need to do is send blood samples to a DNA profiling lab to receive a report with our genomic analysis, and details of diseases we might be at risk of. But what about the damage being done to our systems by pollution, bad habits, mental agony and environmental factors?

The only answer I have is, technology may increase our lifespan, but our bodies are bound to degenerate with time. However, when knowledge joins correct perception, intention and action, there shall be health, wealth and wisdom.

All awareness, consciousness or enlightenment starts in the body. No amount of spiritual knowledge or abundance of wealth is of any use, if we are not healthy. Make peace with your body, listen to it, and become sensitive to its needs, because aside from our innate intelligence and intrinsic healing abilities, it requires our love, care and appreciation. Only then will we be able to go beyond to begin the journey into a state of nirvana, and reach the spiritual zone of self-transcendence.

Life to be alive – needs existence.
Existence to be alive – needs desires.
Desires to be alive – need ego.
Ego to be alive – needs thoughts.
Thoughts to be alive – need awareness.

Chapter 16
Know Thyself

I HAVE MENTIONED BEFORE that the last person we know on earth is our own self. How can we know the self when the inner person does not match the public persona; when we are changing constantly through our choices, dualities and inner conflicts? We can learn about the whole world without ever knowing the self. In fact, other people seem to have a more accurate impression of us than we do ourselves.

The phrase – '*Know thyself*', is inscribed in golden letters in the forecourt of the Apollo temple in Delphi, Greece. Thousands of years have passed but this exhortation still rings true. It remains the *mantra* of gurus and spiritual leaders. Each of us hides behind our dual personalities, within the spheres of good, bad and ugly, but we are not ready to admit this to ourselves. Knowing the self is linked to that part of our character which gives us an accurate representation of our true self. If one wishes to know oneself clearly and completely, the proper way is to first get to know the truth that lies within us. This can be accomplished with inner honesty and devoid of self-judgment.

Moreover, being and knowing oneself is intricately connected. Most of us are not ready to admit that most of what we think and do is imposed upon us by others – parents, teachers, preachers, gurus, spouse, friends, teachers, etc. We must truthfully admit to whether our intentions are guided by others or by the subtle voice within. As Benjamin Franklin said: *'Father of light thou God Supreme – teach me what is good, teach me thyself.'* John Keats said the same thing in other words: *'"Beauty is truth, truth beauty," – that is all / Ye know on earth, and all ye need to know.'*

Truth is precise, indisputable and objective. One has to understand the depth of our truth, reality and intentions – the three secrets to following the supreme command to *'Know thyself'*. Let us probe these three secrets.

Our existence as we know, thrives on dualities, we have lies as a partner to the truth. The truth usually hurts; hence, the foundation on which we continue to live is based on lies. If the truth in us was pure, it would make us absolute in the form of God, which we all know is not the case. Normally a ratio of 30% truth to 70% lies exists. The moment we begin going beyond this level of truth/untruth, there is a transformation; we become aware, conscious and enlightened to that proportionate degree in *'knowing thyself'*. The first secret therefore, is what degree of truth we have within us. This will not only teach us to know ourselves but also become a part of 'being thyself '. In reality, we are a part of 'Thou art That'; we exist both in the worldly self and the divine self, clearly emphasizing the importance of both.

In reality, none of us wants to know the truth. Truth frightens and hurts both the speaker and the listener. We create a facade through which we are lying every moment, starting with social courtesies; spouting phrases like 'thank you', 'sorry', 'it's my pleasure', 'nice to meet you', etc. even when we don't mean them.

Throughout our childhoods, we are taught, numerous behavioural patterns by our parents to safeguard their interests. As we grow and mature, an inner desire should arise to face this world with as much truth as possible, and remove the mask of this false life and its illusions.

Coming to the second secret, it lies in the transformation of energy into matter, to any physical form, and then back into energy – the limitless energy or absolute reality; that reality which is eternal, unchangeable, without distortion or distinctions in time, space or individuality. This absolute reality is, that we all come from one source and dissolve into the same source; like water or its vapour, which originates from the ocean, forming all sorts of shapes from waves to rivers, with different volumes in a limited time frame, but which eventually flows back into its source, the ocean.

Reality can be divided into three levels. The first is illusory reality, which comprises imagination, or hallucinations that exist only in the mind, but which are taken to be real. The second is, relative reality, the zone in which we all exist, because to live, everything has to be related to, or evaluated against its opposite. Here, whatever exists is apparently real, yet not real. The absolute reality is that, which is like the sky or the ocean, having no connection to time or space, and which does not change.

Similarly, the truth of God and us is the same, coming from the same creation, source or energy. Where the divine is in the form of absolute awareness and limitless energy, and we, as the material cause, comprise of the same energy in a limited form, in various frequencies and vibrations. For example, both ocean and waves are part of the same creation – water. A wave has no independent existence; it depends entirely on water; but water can be free from that wave. Water is the material cause of the wave; it becomes a part of and comprises the wave, but is not the wave in reality.

Similarly, God too, is a part of the same creation or energy, complete in awareness. We, in material form within that creation, are sustained in limited form, in relativity, temporarily changing from time to time, and finally ascending back into limitless energy. God, however, is also a part of the same creation, and in absolute reality remains forever in limitless energy, leaving as legacy those who reached that final stage like the Buddha, Lord Jesus and Shri Krishna.

It has been explained that limitless energy is absolute, meaning God and I are the same, and from this energy, both the absolute/relative and subject/object are born. Similarly, when love or truth shines in an objective way, meaning without the duality of hatred and lies, then it reaches the stage of absolute reality, with complete awareness.

This enlightenment is mainly to understand the concept of God, even if we never reach this flow of limitless energy. This makes us aware at least, of the concept of reality within us, in our journey of realization towards the truth.

The third secret, from the level of truth and reality within us, revolves around our intent and its intensity. This power within us exercises whatever degree of truth or reality there is, and illuminates to others and ourselves our true identity. This hidden intention is the sum of our self and its shadow. As we proceed in our journey towards knowing ourselves, the power of our intention delivers energy for us to reach the basic truth.

What is it that we really want from life and to what lengths are we prepared to go – consciously, subconsciously or unconsciously – in achieving our goals? The more we know and accept the truth within us, the stronger the power of our intention and realization.

All of us, with intellect and technology, obtain knowledge to specialize in our respective fields. However, amongst all the branches of knowledge, there is one that each of us has to be aware of, where we have no choice. That is Self-knowledge, knowing that the mind is not us and the ego is the false self. The real 'us' is the subtle witnessing Self, which on being aware becomes conscious to form your consciousness.

We may excel in whatever we do, but our life is wasted if we are unable to discover the truth about ourselves, as then we would be perennially confused and dissatisfied. This may sound easy, but our mind plays multiple tricks to keep us in the dark about the realization and awareness of our inner truth. Eastern philosophy clearly dictates that one must know the true Self, because the self is your only permanent friend, yet at the same time, it can be one's foe, if not fully understood.

Last but not least, learn how to love yourself. Love is the truth and reality of life. Love can be obtained only through awareness of our real being. Be aware of the body – the divine resides within. Be aware of the mind, where the consciousness within determines what we are. Be aware of awareness, where our intentions determine the presence of who we are.

Acknowledgements

I am indebted to the following people:

Friends and family members, who encouraged me at every step, indulging me during my lengthy monologues on the subject of Spirituality. Their invaluable critiques helped me tide over doubts and rough stages during the writing process;

My Editors, for improving form and content, and patiently re-reading drafts of the manuscript;

To my wife Komilla Kumar, thank you for your patience, love, support and inspiration.

To my children, Nadisha Gulati and Shreeya Kumar Bhola, who will always be my creative force.

Finally, I dedicate this in memory of my parents, my greatest inspiration, for making me who I am today.

Notes

Wish To Publish With Us?

We are always keen to look at interesting content across genres. Please email your submission to: **submissions@leadstartcorp.com**

The submission should include the following:

1. Synopsis

A summary of the book in 500 – 1000 words. Please mention the word count of the manuscript.

2. Sample chapters

Two chapters, not necessarily in order; just send the two best.

3. A Note About The Author

An interesting note about yourself (about 200 words).

4. Additional Information

- Target audience,
- Unique selling points
- List of illustrative content (if any)
- Other comparative titles
- Your thoughts on marketing the book.

Notes